Graphics In InDesign

Graphics in

InDesign

VECTOR ILLUSTRATION

Typographic Manipulation

David Bergsland

Radiqx PRESS
MANKATO, MINNESOTA

ISBN-13: 978-1492119630

ISBN-10: 1492119636

Published by Radiqx Press, Mankato, Minnesota
Contact: info@radiqx.com or http://bergsland.org

Dedicated to fellow book creators who
may not realize how well InDesign draws

Contents

Using InDesign produce graphics?

Yes, that is what I'm suggesting. More and more I hear designers talking about how InDesign has become the drawing software we lost when FreeHand was done away with. In this little book, you will discover that it is very easy to quickly make a PDF graphic in InDesign while working on your book. The cover of this little booklet was produced completely in InDesign with the addition of a few paths pasted in from old FreeHand drawings. It's all vectors.

Can you guess which ones are FreeHand?

The word InDesign was traced from a hand-drawn marker script. The butterfly was laid back in perspective in Free-Hand many years ago: Beside those two, everything was drawn in InDesign. The effects [embossing and things like that] were applied in InDesign to the words: InDesign, & Typographic Manipulation, VECTOR ILLUSTRATION. The Screen Mode applied to the arc was done in InDesign. It all went quite fast. I'm talking a few minutes once I had the pieces assembled.

More than that all the typographic effects are applied to live type. The type can still be edited like normal type!

InDesign has many of the important Illustrator and Photoshop tools built in. But we will talk about that as we go. You will still need Photoshop to crop, sharpen, adjust levels, and all the others things which need to be done for photos. You'll especially need Photoshop to rasterize the PDFs used for print into JPEGs used for ePUBs.

But the bottom line is that I have a copy of Illustrator—in fact I have the entire CC package of apps, plus the CS6 Web & Design Premium Suite. I keep several of them installed out of habit, but all I use are Acrobat, Bridge, Photoshop, & InDesign. And I use old versions of everything except InDesign.

Image production in InDesign

One of the real benefits of writing and assembling your book in InDesign is that it is also an excellent graphic production tool. There is nothing better for the production of your cover—especially in print where you need the front cover, back cover and spine all in one image produced to exacting size restrictions. In addition, it is an excellent tool for graphs, charts, maps, and the rest of your needs for graphics in your books. I'll discuss cover designs at the end of book production.

But for now, you need to understand that image production has become much more complex with the addition of the ebook formats. There are radical differences between what is needed for print and what is needed for an ePUB or Kindle book. You have many options for graphics. What I want to do is explain these options and show you how to deal with them.

 The changing standards: The ebook standards are in constant flux. The good news is that ePUB and KF8 (the latest Kindle format for the Kindle Fire) have become close enough so that the graphic standards are nearly identical. However, the new iPad has doubled the resolution available for ePUBs. But the Fire HD comes close as do other Android tablets. But little of this has changed anything so far as the high resolution images carry way too much file size to be practical for a book like this and Kindle still limits graphic size to 127K. In print, it's 300 dpi CMYK.

The hidden truth: InDesign is the best replacement for FreeHand

Back a decade or so, there were two professional illustration programs: FreeHand & Illustrator. Adobe bought FreeHand and killed it. It was the best and easiest to use illustration application, especially for typographic illustrations. As Ole Kvern and I commented a while back on one of the InDesign lists, InDesign is the best replacement for FreeHand. For simple graphics, logos, and typographic illustrations, InDesign is far superior to Illustrator. If you are not a professional illustrator, InDesign is better for you.

InDesign makes superior PDFs for print, and they are very easy to rasterize to size in Photoshop to use in ebooks. In fact, all my illustrations are done in InDesign and Photoshop. They are drawn as needed while I write my books. InDesign makes wonderful maps and floor plans for my novels, as an example.

Adding graphics to your book

Here we have a real problem. Graphics in Word are not usable professionally. In fact, in many cases Word cannot even add professional graphics to a Word document. Print graphics are vector (PDFs, EPSs, or AI files) or bitmap (Photoshop files, photographs, and the like). Bitmap files must be 300 dpi.

More than that, photos must be sharp, in focus, with good contrast. They should be CMYK (the color space of print). Even though some on-demand printers now use RGB images, the colors will change when they are converted to CMYK for printing.

But for most of your printing, your graphics will be high resolution grayscale—so you will need to store high resolution color versions for conversion to use in your ebooks. We will talk about this in much greater depth later in the book. But I must mention a few things here.

One of the most obvious areas of amateurism is found in the images many self publishers use to promote and market their books. Even worse are some of the graphics I have seen used inside of these books. Many of them are so blurry they cannot be read. Even if they are not blurry, they are commonly quite ugly and of poor quality.

You must use professional grade images. Traditionally an excellent professional photo cost around $300 for a single use. The truly superb images still cost that much. But in most cases, those prices are long gone. But you must be careful to get images for which you have a legal license.

Many of these stock photo companies also offer professional quality vector graphic also. This is what you will need for those maps in the front of your novels, for example. I'll show you what a vector graphic is in a couple of pages down the road.

Using Photos (the most common graphics used)

The best solution here is to use photos you have shot with a good digital camera. Images from your smart phone will probably not do. The problem is that printing quality requires 300 dpi. That can be hard to find. For example, images in this book are usually five inches wide or more. That means I must have images which are 1500 pixels wide or better—after cropping.

You can also use royalty-free images from the Web that give you free rights to publish as you wish. There are many sources for images like these. Wikimedia Commons is good—as is MorgueFile. Sites like Fotolia offer professional quality images at very reasonable prices. Just make sure you read the rights copy carefully. Many images have some restrictions, even if it is only adding a Photo Credit line next to your image. Just make sure they are large enough in pixel dimensions and in color.

JPEGs: You need to be very careful with JPEGs. The method of compression uses averages where you are not only lossy (image data is deleted), but they also have bad artifacts around all the contrasty edges of the image. These can actually destroy the image beyond usability. Above you can see an example of extreme JPEG compression:

The images above are twice the resolution (if your ereader can show those differences). Even here a lot of the damage looks very small. However, at 72 dpi (what you need for the Web and for ebooks), the image on the right page is completely unusable except as a bad example. But they are in color and that helps a lot. Plus a Retina Display can work wonders. Maybe they both look equally bad in an ereader, but in print they're horrible and the JPEG is much worse.

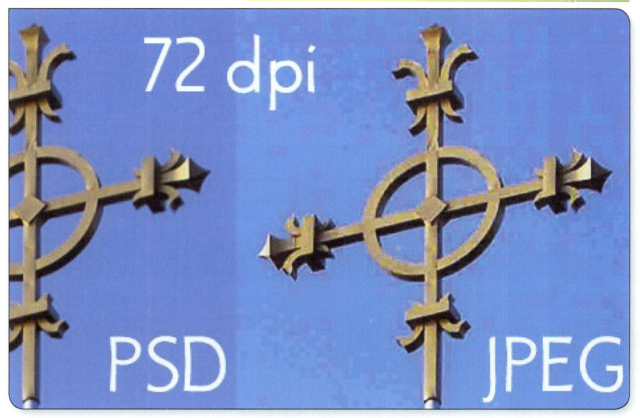

Using drawings & paintings

Paintings are done in Photoshop (or converted in Photoshop), so they have the same resolution problems as we see above. For now, you'll just have to take my word for it about the quality of the 600 pixel wide ebook images. We'll talk about it more in the sections on ebook conversions.

Scanned art: this would include scanned pencil drawings, inkwork, or anything else. As soon as it is scanned the identical resolution and JPEG artifact issues arise.

Vector art [the native output of Illustrator and InDesign]: Because vector files can be resized with no problems and rasterized at any size or resolution you need, you can have one graphic master file for all your needs in the various formats. It is also much easier to change color spaces with vector images—especially if you are using InDesign for your drawings. The Swatches panel in InDesign makes conversions like this very easy—as long as you have sense enough to have a predefined color palette.

Vector versus bitmap

I do not expect you to forget about the bitmapped extravaganzas commonly developed in Photoshop. However, developing excellent type illustrations in InDesign and then rasterizing them in Photoshop will give you much better typographic control of your graphics. I will talk about this process later in the book.

Vector drawing is one of the most misunderstood tools in our arsenal. Digital drawing, sometimes known as PostScript illustration, is one of the indispensable tools of digital publishing. However, it has been lost in the hype of smart phones and digital cameras. Back in the bad ol'days (before computers), when we >gasp< had to do everything by hand, things were clearer. There was camerawork, inkwork, typesetting, and pasteup. These areas have been replaced by image manipulation, digital drawing, word processing, and page layout software. InDesign does all of these except for camerawork and image manipulation. Camerawork and image manipulation are the purpose of Photoshop.

With vector graphics, we are now talking about inkwork instead of camerawork—digital drawing instead of image manipulation. What does that mean? It means that we are looking at an entirely different type of artwork. This artwork is not focused on soft transitions and subtle effects. The purpose of this type of art is fundamentally different. These are images that are crisp, precise, and direct. This is where we leave the natural world and enter an environment with no dirt, no scratches, no broken parts, no garbage.

Let's start with an actual graphic ◇◇◇◇◇◇◇◇

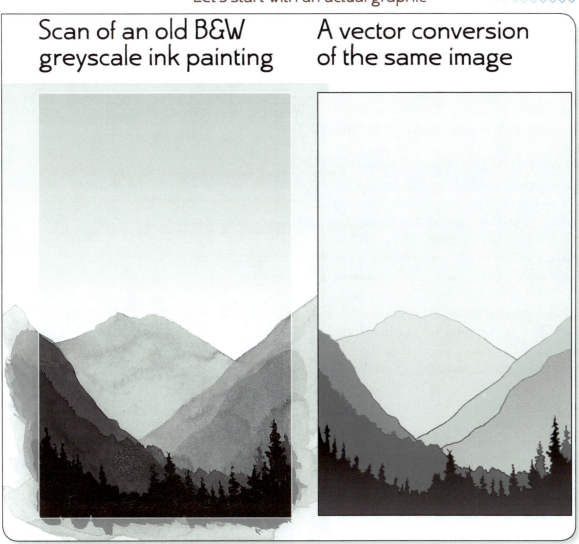

Scan of an old B&W
greyscale ink painting

A vector conversion
of the same image

It is obvious that vector drawing is very different from a painting, photograph, or any other scanned object. It's not to say that one is better than the other—they are simply different. The painting is soft, subtle, more "realistic." The vector drawing is clean, crisp, easily resizable, with a much smaller file size.

It is also extremely easy to add professional-quality, easily resizable type to a vector drawing. Any type added to the original painting must be drawn by hand. Even if you are working with a scan of the art in Photoshop, type is limited to large point sizes and fuzzy edges. Photoshop type needs 1200 dpi to 2400 dpi to be sharp enough for printing.

As you can see to the right, the vector landscape from the previous page can be easily resized and have type added to it. There is no fuzziness or pixelation. The type is crisp and sharp, even if it were printed out at 500% of the original size of the drawing. If this were a Photoshop file, it would be pixelated here. By pixelated, we mean that you could see the jagged edges of the individual picture elements or pixels.

Finally, the Photoshop type would be very crude at 200 to 300 dots per inch, whereas the vector graphic has type at the typographic standard—1,200 dpi to 2,400 dpi (or whatever the resolution of the printer

is). Imagine if we printed it out at two foot wide or more. The vector image would still be sharp.

Below we see the vector version enlarged 600%. You can see some of the drawing deficiencies, but the image is still crisp. The same would be true if we enlarged it to hang as a billboard on the side of a skyscraper at 50 yards wide. There would be no pixilization.

However, that sharpness is not true of scanned, or bitmapped, images: The Photoshop (bitmapped) version is ruined at two feet wide, as you can see below. When the image was enlarged to two feet wide, the pixels could not change shape. So, we now see what that bitmap really looked like.

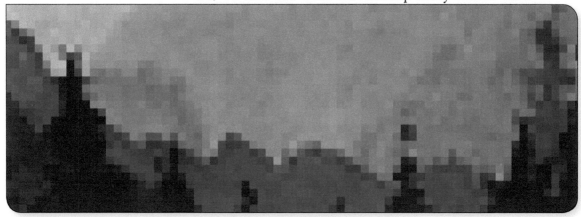

The only reason it looked smooth was that the pixels were a three hundredth of an inch each and that is far too small to be seen. In the enlargement, the pixels are nearly an eighth of an inch square and easily visible. Also this enlarged bitmapped image was 235 MB. Full page high resolution full color images like you use on your covers are often 25 MB or more. If You use many of these images in a book like this one, the file size gets huge.

The vector image remains 49 KB no matter what size you use for output. Yes, that is 235 million bytes as compared to 49 thousand bytes of data. Obviously, there are some real advantages to vector illustration.

There are two major advantages to vector art: ◇◇◇◇◇◇

- **It is completely resizable:** Vector art is what is commonly referred to as *resolution independent*. There is no resolution to a vector file. All of the shapes, and this includes all the type, are defined by mathematical outlines that can be enlarged or reduced at will. The resolution is produced by the printer, screen, or Photoshop.

- **The file size is normally much smaller:** This is not always the case with very complicated vector images. However, the 49K versus 235MB comparison is very common.

This means that I can make my original artwork for the first version of the book and then easily resize, recolor, and convert it into any file type, size, and resolution needed for the rest of the versions.

I can open it in Photoshop and convert it to 72 dpi (rasterize it) at the size needed for the JPEGs, GIFs, and PNGs needed for Kindle or ePUBs. I can enlarge the image to a poster or book cover and/or reduce the size to a ding-bat used for bulleted lists all from the same original. This cannot be done with a bitmapped image.

InDesign produces excellent vector images. We'll cover some techniques later on in the book. Your concern, at this point, is to make sure all of the images you use are of professional quality. You cannot use Web images for print.

The lizard was an old FreeHand drawing, but I gave up on fixing it in Illustrator and colorized it in InDesign. It was simply too difficult to work on it within Illustrator.

The fastest and most common graphic

Speed is one of the reasons to use words as graphics. However, this does not touch on the real reason why words are most commonly used for graphics. To cover that reason, it is helpful to remember that old saying attributed to some ancient Chinese wise man, "A picture is worth a thousand words." Actually it sounds more like Shakespeare, but it makes no real difference. There is really a major problem with that old proverb. A picture does indeed speak volumes. The problem is found in controlling (or even predicting) what the image talks about.

I am not saying that an accurately directed, impeccably crafted illustration is not a wonder — and extremely effective. The problems are the normal ones: time and money. Now, you may be one of those incredibly talented (and fortunate) designers who wind up working for a superstar publisher as one of their primo talents. Then you don't have to concern yourself about those two little worries just mentioned.

Just listen, then, while the rest of us talk about the real world of illustration and digital graphics. In self publishing, the margins are real tight. Kawasaki in *APE* talks about the need to sell 2500 books to make a profit with base costs of several thousand dollars. That's all very nice, but I don't have anywhere near that kind of budget and my niches are normally too small to support that many sales. I need graphics I can do for free [or close to it]. In addition, they must be professional to avoid the need to lower prices because my quality is so low. The result of all of this is that graphic treatments of words will regularly be the solution of choice.

The frequency of this choice is increased by the simple fact that often there is no real graphic conceivable to describe what you really need to help sell that book about the joys of service, the need for faith, or that support book for your seminars offering help with Depression. Words are clear, concise, and can be graphically strong.

Words are direct and precise

When you really need it, and can say it accurately, what works better than **FREE**? How about a snappy graphic saying whatever you need? The plug-in graphic below would not make a good headline or logo; it's not strong enough. But it certainly adds interest as a subhead on a page where some sort of graphic is visually necessary. It could be used as a subhead or an added illustration—even a drop cap graphic.

In general, you will find many occasions when a quick graphic made of words will solve your graphic dilemma handily. Often you don't even have to write those words — they are offered as part of the story you are writing. So, what we want to do here is give you

the tools and structure to effectively use words as graphics. What we need to do now is give you conceptual control of what you have been doing.

There is no such thing as a bad font

Your main task is to pick fonts that are appropriate in style and readable. You have a huge variety to choose from. In fact, a large part of your personal design style will be the font library you build. This is something to start working on now. Do not just pick styles that you like. There are too many instances in which a type style that you find abhorrent is the perfect solution to a design need for a particular client's readership.

But enough talk, let's look at a real project [I redid an old FreeHand in InDesign and it is much better quality]. I have a little type foundry that sells type online. I needed a small graphic, almost a logo, to identify the foundry. All I had was the name, NuevoDeco Typography, and a strong sense that the logostyle should use only the fonts from the foundry. I started with the word portion, DECO. I wanted it to be dominant, so I used one of my fonts called Adept-Heavy (I no longer sell this one).

Because I wanted this word fragment to be a solid unit, I tracked and kerned it tightly. I deleted some of the excessive Celtic flares. The even/odd overlap of the D and E had to be eliminated, so I subselected the two outlines and used the Add command. Finally, I filled the entire word fragment with a gradient and added a quarter-point stroke to lighten it a little. Now the four letters looked

like a unit. You would probably do it much differently. That'
fine. I would also now 20 years later.

Next I added the word *typogra-*
phy. I must have used five or ten different fonts. They were all too stylized
for this location, so I finally settled on
Nördström Black Nördström is conservative—yet friendly and seems to fit the
need well.

The word fragment *Nuevo*, in contrast, needed more
style, almost a handwritten look. Of course, I had the
option to use handwriting. However, I was limiting myself
to NuevoDeco fonts. So I chose one of my nostalgic fonts
from the fifties, AeroScript.

I had to do what I did with DECO here also. The word
is skewed and scaled; converted to outlines; ungrouped and
the paths split; all of the outside shapes were made into
one path with the Unite command. Then I subtracted the
counters of the e and o. and the word was joined together
again with a light basic fill and the half-point stroke.

Because I needed a small graphic for my Web page,
I decided that I needed a frame to hold the graphic. So, I
dropped a round-cornered box with vertical gradient (because
it compresses better) behind the words. I added quite a bit
of color. However, the color made the word *TYPOGRAPHY*
disappear into the background, so I added a one-point white
stroke around it.

Finally, I took the DECO art and added some fun
effects to it, debossing it into the surface and playing with
the color to get enough contrast to make it all readable.

The whole process took an hour or two. I think it
accurately gives a sense of my typographic style in the mid-
1990s and shows off three of my fonts which I was selling
at the time. I wouldn't do it the same now, of course.

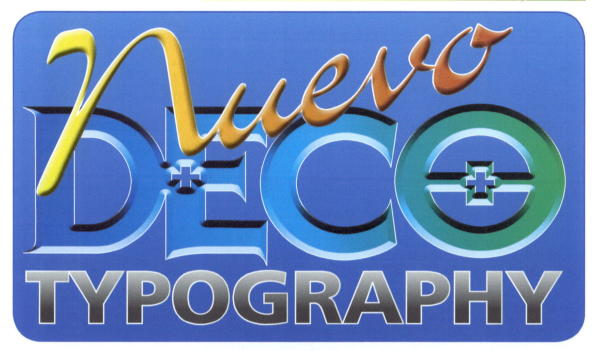

Nuevo DECO TYPOGRAPHY

What is an appropriate font?

Stop

PERFUME
EAU DE PARIS

Or

      In general, you have to define that. There is a general sense of what works and what doesn't. The stop sign on the left would be proof of that. It's doubtful that the logo next to it would sell much $300-per-ounce perfume either [though I've seen something similar for some "manly" cologne]. Sometimes type usage is this obvious. Most of the time it is not. Normally you have to come up with a general sense of the style of type that appeals to the readership of your particular project and accurately conveys the style of the place and culture being talked about in your book.

This is something you need to train your eye to recognize. You can get a feel for this by watching television show openers that are targeted at specific demographics. There is a large difference in the style of type used by RFD-TV and A&E or Bravo, for instance. Hawaii 50 has a very distinct typographic style that is very different from Two and a Half Men. It's fascinating to observe the continuous differences between Fox News Network and CNN in all areas.

Another area to watch is fashion retailers. In New Mexico, for example, the extremely expensive, high-fashion boutiques in Santa Fe around the Plaza use very different typestyles from the malls in Albuquerque. The malls are much closer to the national usage found on TV in ads for The Limited, Eddie Bauer, Sears, Penneys, and other national chains. Austin will have a different style from Dallas or Houston. San Francisco is different from LA is different from Seattle. If you want to see a clear regional style that has spread worldwide, look at Starbucks, from Seattle. You will not only have to educate yourself, you will have to continuously feed your eye and your mind with current images for the rest of your career. It's part of being a writer.

More to the point, genre covers: We have to see what our genre uses. A political/military thriller for example almost certainly needs the White House, Congress, presidential seal, CIA seal, or something similar. A romance? Two or three people large with a scene from the locale of the book in the background is usually standard. *Angie's Decision*, as seen on the opposite page, would probably not do well as a romance cover. The same applies to non-fiction, reference, or any type of book. You need to spend some time browsing in your local bookstore and in the online stores. Interior graphics also have a style for different types of books: fantasy maps, for example.

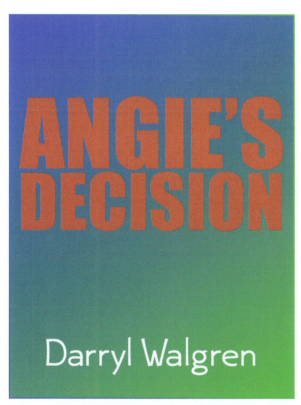

ANGIE'S DECISION

Darryl Walgren

The bottom line? A book designer is a graphic designer

That is a simple fact which many new self publishing authors fail to take into account. Once they self publish they are responsible for the graphic excellence of their books, as much as they are for the written content. You have two choices: you can do it yourself or you can pay someone else to do it. Regardless, it must be done.

Some basic guidelines

Now that I have given you one of my examples, we can probably talk a little more clearly about basic typographic choices. When you first begin, choosing an appropriate font runs into two problems: "I really like that one," or, "Oh my gosh, which one is the right choice?" To rephrase, you tend to pick fonts because you like them or you're unable to choose because of all the choices (and you might be wrong).

The first option: your personal taste

When you begin as a designer, this is almost always the wrong choice. Your eye is not educated enough to have good taste. Your personal font favorites are appropriate only when you are a member of the readership. Like everyone else, your taste is a result of your personal experiences: cultural, academic, social, and political. If you are less than sixty years of age, your typographic choices are greatly affected by the television shows you have been watching since youth. They have been trained by ads for the Gap, Millers Outpost, Levi's, Sears, L. L. Bean, or wherever you buy your clothes.

Unknowingly, you have been herded into a demographic grouping (even if that grouping is *the rebellious ones*). I remember one of my more talented students, whose entire existence was colored by the graphics and lifestyle of snowboarders. He kept talking about the typographic freedom his group used, and how he wanted to design for them. It was a massive comedown when he realized how rigid the graphic style was that had been used to appeal to him and his "buds."

It took almost two terms before he realized that the "freedom" he was so excited about was really a very rigid style. The rule was simple: "Break all the rules!" He eventually became an excellent typographer once he realized that he had an easier time than most understanding normal usage. It was simply the absolute opposite of his group's norms. If he liked sans serif body copy, the norm is serif. He found that he could effectively design for very conservative clients by simply choosing the opposite of his natural inclinations.

The problem with personal taste is personal experience

It took me several years to grasp why my clients, students, and readers always seemed to pick my least favorite choice when I gave them a set of options for a logo or layout. Over the years, I have listened to countless book designers who were virtually spitting on the people commenting on prospective covers, *"They picked the ugliest one. I almost didn't include it. I should have tossed it."* Then one day I realized, while doing a flyer project for a client, that the one

Futura: This font family is commonly chosen by the ignorant.

AaBbCcDd
EeFfGgHhIiJj
KkLlMmNn
OoPpQqRr
SsTtUuVvWw
XxYyZz1234
567890

But it's not readable: You really need to be careful with your font choices.

I liked best simply reminded me of some of the posters I had designed for my rock group back in Minneapolis in the 1960s. It had nothing to do with good taste. It was all about happy personal experiences.

Since then, I have seen countless examples of designers who made absolute statements of taste and style based on good memories of former times. You are also strongly colored by bad periods of your life. For example, the Retro fad of sixties nostalgia triggered many horrible memories in me and all of my friends. You will never convince me that stuff from the fifties or sixties has any value at all. Mid-century modern? Give me a break! I have spent much of my life fighting that culture and mentality.

Our personal tastes are all based on those types of emotional reactions to fonts, colors, layouts, styles, and so forth. We have to train ourselves to recognize the difference between merely personal taste and genuine excellence in design — between personal taste and truly ugly graphics. More than that, we have to learn what appeals to various cultural subgroups and readerships. For example, I know that the group known as the Spanish (in New Mexico, as distinct from Mexican or Latino or Chicano—though including all three) was strongly attracted by Art Nouveau fonts in the 1980s. This probably has little to do with similar ethnic subgroups with different titles in Southern California or Miami, but it certainly worked around there. This is what you have to learn. I just designed a book for a couple who had spent a decade ministering to the street children of Acapulco. They loved the Art Nouveau type I used. I didn't.

You must learn your local culture. We were strongly, and proudly, multicultural in New Mexico, but it was entirely Anglo, Spanish, and Indian. Now that I'm back in Minnesota, the culture defines multicultural in terms of the Somalis, Hmong, Blacks, and Mexicans who live around the small farming city I live in. There was a strong Japanese influence that I really liked in Oregon, especially around Eugene where I was living.

You must become intimately familiar with the graphic heritage of your area and your genre. It's a language you have to speak fluently. The America culture has become too diverse to pin down. You need to discover the visual language of your readership. Look at books sold to your readership—especially the really popular ones. As mentioned, for genre of military/political thrillers, the cover almost requires a presidential seal, the White House, or the Capital Building to reach the normal readership.

The second problem: overwhelmed by choices ◇◇◇◇◇

One of the major problems faced by my students was their reaction to the font list I give them at the beginning of every term. I have about 5,000 fonts, and I printed out a restricted list of the 300 or so that I made available on all the computers in my lab. This list varied yearly, with new fonts added and ones I was bored with removed. However, the reaction was usually the same.

Most new designers (and self publishers) are overwhelmed by the choices. Beyond that, they can hardly see the differences between Baskerville, Garamond, and Caslon. It is always fascinating to watch who chooses which fonts to use in their projects. When I start explaining why Avant Garde or Helvetica is a bad choice for body copy, for instance, they fall into bewilderment. They plaintively ask, "How do I know?" The fact is that it is fairly easy to learn to make good font choices, but it takes a bit of effort.

The best way I know is to immerse yourself in excellent design to the national market. Communicating graphically to the entire nation requires two things. First of all, you have to avoid all local stylistic distinctions. Secondly, you have to make excellent, classic typographic choices to avoid boredom in your more generic audience.

You also see it every day in the traditionally published books you read. If you are reading cheap Kindle books, you may have a problem. You need to look for excellent, well-designed books and magazines. I would suggest going to your local book superstore and perusing the magazines and the best-selling books. This time, avoid those that really appeal to you. I am always sucked in by Taunton Press and Fine Gardening, Fine Woodworking, and the rest of their line, for example. They are excellent and a good source of graphic style. However, for our purpose here, you need to inspect Look, People, Times, Newsweek, and magazines designed to appeal to the mass market of North America. There are similar publications in New Zealand, Australia, Europe, and Southeast Asia. Currently there are massive numbers of specialty magazines—one or more of which are targeted directly at your readership. These magazines, and the people who advertise in them, have made a science out of typography that offends no one yet remains interesting and visually appealing. Look at the two music channel logos to the left. They're obviously going for different niches.

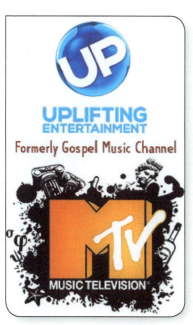

Study the books in your genre or target market. Examine their basic layouts. Which fonts do they use? How are they structured? Look at ads for the major car companies and ask the same questions. Closely analyze advertising from Procter and Gamble, Sears, Wal-Mart, and others that have made such an impact on our national graphic taste. The people who design for them often have research budgets that would make us blush (or turn green). They rarely use type styles by whim or by accident. Take their ads and try to match the fonts used to your font lists. If you have few choices, at least get a good font catalog from Adobe, ITC, Agfa, or Bitstream.

Build off these choices. The classics will almost always work and work well. In general, the fancy decorative fonts are used only for the most prominent headlines or logo-styles. Most of you will have at least one of the Garamond families or Caslon. Once you learn how to handle one font family well, it is much easier to move on to other fonts. It is a marvelous exercise to design complete documents with only one font in various sizes of caps, small caps, and cap/lowercase. Beyond that, the use of only one font is often an extremely elegant solution to the graphic needs of a book.

Drawing in InDesign

Why would you ever want to draw in InDesign? Better tools and unique capabilities are the answers: While it is true that InDesign has a very limited set of Illustrator's tools, it uses them in a much better interface. True, InDesign is not a true, full-featured illustration program. However, most book graphics do not require or even want the full features of blends, gradients meshes, perspective, and the rest of the fancier Illustrator capabilities. Most book illustrations are relatively simple tables, and line art info graphics. While it may be true that Illustrator can do them better, Illustrator greatly adds to your learning burden as a writer in InDesign. If you have Illustrator skills, certainly use them. But do not think they are required.

Why you want to make graphics in InDesign

One of the little secrets in digital publishing in recent years is the fact that increasing numbers of designers are using InDesign for all of their graphic production except for photographs and scans. InDesign's drawing interface is uncluttered and works remarkably well. The primary reasons for using InDesign to draw are the seven we list beginning on the next spread. But the real issue goes much deeper than that. Unless you are a professional illustrator the drawing capabilities of Adobe's Illustrator are far too complex and take too much time to be used in book production.

Typographic graphics:

The core of my reasoning is simple. The graphics which are not photos are usually (often, at least) type. Even the pieces built around photos are commonly made with a lot of type. You do not want to make these images in Photoshop because the type will end up rasterized at far too low a resolution. As I have said, type for print is normally output at 2400 dpi or at least 1200 dpi for the cheaper technologies. Photoshop images are 300 dpi, at best. The result is that type in Photoshop images is pretty chewed up. The only way type in Photoshop works well is if it is larger than 18 point.

It is true that you can save Photoshop graphics that contain high resolution type—but our on-demand suppliers cannot handle that (at this point). For our purposes, Photoshop is a bitmap application, working in pixels that are precisely defined. Photoshop is a tool you will need to learn (at least in a minimal manner) to handle many things in on-demand publishing—it's one of the very few which can work in CMYK, for example. Even Photoshop Elements cannot work in CMYK. The bad news is that this powerful capability to render very tiny pixels with a great deal of control is also its greatest limitation.

The good news is that InDesign has all you need to produce beautiful graphics.

In fact, it has several attributes that lead me to create most of my graphics within InDesign, because in these areas InDesign is definitely superior to either Illustrator or Photoshop. There is nothing better for assembling graphics from different pieces: drawings, photos, and type. I have mentioned several of these abilities already, but they center around three basic capabilities: type, color, and PDFs.

> **Typography:** Nothing else comes close. It is easier and better, in most cases, to do all your type in InDesign. Even when you are tearing type apart to make logos and graphics, InDesign is easier and faster than Illustrator in many cases. It can do many things with

type that are impossible in Photoshop—
simply because InDesign creates vector art.

🌹 **Live stylized type:** In InDesign you can do
anything to the type short of tearing apart
the individual outline or using Pathfinder
operations while the type remains editable.
This includes gradient strokes or fills,
and any of the Photoshop Effects.

🌹 **Color control:** No other program has the color
palette control of the Swatches panel in InDesign.
Nowhere is it more easy to build a predetermined
custom palette for a specific project. You can
easily control the color of a large project like a
book in InDesign (and keep control across all the
various formats). This is much more difficult in
Illustrator and almost impossible in Photoshop.

🌹 **Gradient strokes:** This seems like a little thing,
but it is huge. Many typographic decorations
like rules are simply lines. Only InDesign
can make gradient lines easily. Plus, these
gradient lines remain editable. Any gradient
in Photoshop requires rasterized art and type.
*[Yes, I know that Illustrator CS6 has finally
added gradient strokes. But, as usual, the
implementation is so complex that it is daunting.]*

🌹 **Individual corner controls:** Built into every
frame, InDesign has corner controls that allow
you to control all at once as well as each corner
separately—by directly manipulating the frame.

🌹 **Photoshop effects:** Many of the basic effects
(Photoshop styles) are available in InDesign.
The Effects panel is remarkable with individual
controls for the entire vector object (or group
of objects), or only the stroke, only the fill, and
any combination thereof. Drop shadows, inner

shadows, inner glow, outer glow, embossing & debossing, plus transparency feathering are easy to apply. Plus, the type remains editable.

🔶 **PDF generation:** InDesign simply produces the best PDFs. I use InDesign almost exclusively to make PDFs of logos, book covers, product graphics, and all the rest. This is especially true if these graphics must be rasterized into high resolution JPEGs and PNGs for our suppliers.

Createspace covers, for example, demand rasterized artwork. In fact, strange as it may seem, they require a Photoshop PDF—which is very unusual. The InDesign file is much more editable and rasterizing it into Photoshop for Createspace's (Amazon's) purposes is quick & easy. You do not want to be doing your back cover type in Photoshop—even though Createspace requires you to do so.

Type manipulation

This is even more true with typographic art. Digital drawing goes far beyond simple pen work. Its main power is found in type manipulation. One of InDesign's major assets is its ability to rapidly convert a word or two into a powerful graphic very quickly. Of course, there are some major differences between InDesign and traditional drawing. Formerly, we had to hand-draw the line to the proper width. With vector shapes, I can specify any fill with strokes (outlines) of any color or any width—virtually infinite flexibility, with a precision that was incomprehensible

before the late 1980s when the first PostScript drawing programs were released: Fontographer first, followed by Illustrator and then FreeHand. On the opposite page [and below in the sidebar] is a simple one: the Radiqx Press logo—which is two words, a couple gradients, and a cross punched out of the modified R [using the Pathfinder panel in InDesign]. **I drew this in InDesign:** For color the dot over the i is a red radial gradient. For logos there is nothing better. Logos have to be the most flexible graphics imaginable. They will be used very small, very large, and everything in between. There must be black-and-white versions, greyscale versions, process color versions, and in addition, low-resolution RGB Web versions.

Digital drawing using PostScript paths is almost specifically designed for this purpose. InDesign enables very tiny file sizes that are resolution independent. In other words, they will print at the highest resolution allowed by the printing press, printer, or monitor.

The Create Outlines command converts your fonts into a collection of editable shapes. With fonts converted to paths, you can use any font and not have to worry about including it. It is still the best way to get fancy decorative fonts on the Web or into an ebook. Rasterizing your converted type into Photoshop is very easy.

Charts & graphs

Many graphics in common usage are charts and graphs. All of the common software, like spreadsheets and presentation software, produce horrible-looking work that is designed for a monitor. To translate, that means they are in the wrong color space for most color printing and far too low in resolution. Basically, every chart or graph you receive will have to be tossed completely or scanned and used as a rough template in the background while you recreate the graphic to professional standards so you can use it wherever you need it in all of your book formats.

As you can see from the sample showing usage of watercolor board to the right, even the best I can do with the received graphic is terrible. I received the image as a 72 dpi, RGB TIFF generated from a PowerPoint slide. Even for this example, I have done a lot of work in Photoshop: cropping tightly; resizing the image

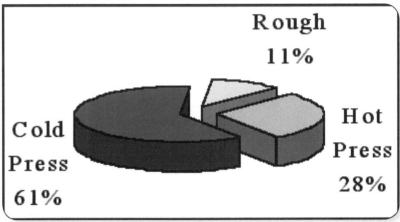

to half size, thereby increasing the resolution to 144 dpi; and converting the image to grayscale.

The result is still hardly inspiring. The font choice is clumsy, at best—not to mention that it does not fit my Styles. The type alignment, leading, tracking, and so on are very amateurish. Worst of all, there is no explanation to help the reader determine if this knowledge is helpful, useful, or even relevant. In all ways, this graphic is useless unless it is used as part of a well-spoken, entertainingly written, enthusiastically presented oral explanation.

We have to remember, as authors and book publishers, that our explanations are found in the professional presentation of our copy. Poor font choices cannot be covered with glib jokes or even pithy commentary. Our readers are going to make choices based on the attractiveness and usefulness of our layouts.

First of all, they will decide whether they are even going to read our work. If it is not clear in concept and easy to comprehend, you have lost them. In your book, you rarely get a second chance. So, with that in mind, let us redesign this awful pie chart.

Before we can start with that, we need to know what it represents: By talking to the client and asking questions, I discover that it refers to the use of watercolor board by the art department of an architectural design firm for the past year. They are in the process of making a presentation package that they can use to show their changing focus and capabilities to prospective investors as the firm expands.

As I learn this, I also find another bar chart showing, paradoxically, that **sales resulting from the use of the boards give a very different view:** The rough board is used for hand-painted gouache illustrations, for which this firm is developing a real reputation. The cold press sheets are used as mounting board for client presentations to use as they seek to fill the spaces of the various projects with targeted tenants. The hot press is used for quick visualizations, models, and as a mounting board for general signage.

It turns out that the expensive d'Arches 300# rough watercolor board is used for illustrations that generate 57% of all income. The cold press board used for client presentations and to present proofs to the clients for printed materials in support of their buildings represents 32% of the income. The hot press board is second as far as expense is concerned, but it only accounts for 11% of the income.

With that in mind, I quickly traced the ugly PowerPoint slide (by hand, using the Pen tool), extending the height of the various slices (adjusting by eye) to Provide the data from the second chart. I then added more stylish type giving both sets of figures; added a title line; and colored in the shapes. It took about a half hour to fix up the graph. However, there is a much greater likelihood that it will actually be read now. More than that, the data now makes an important point which can clearly and easily be seen. I just needed to double-check with the client to make sure it was making the proper emphasis—it was.

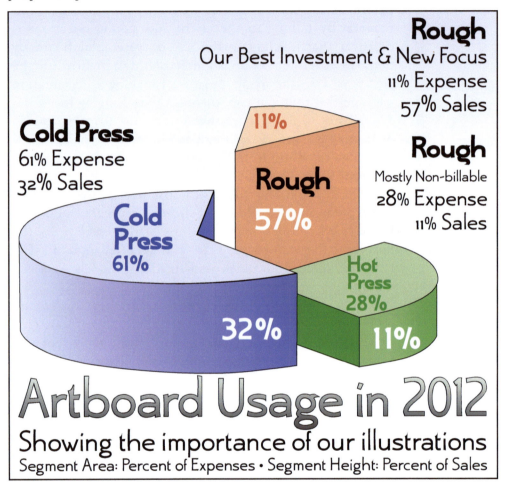

Rough
Our Best Investment & New Focus
11% Expense
57% Sales

Rough
Mostly Non-billable
28% Expense
11% Sales

Cold Press
61% Expense
32% Sales

Cold Press 61%

Rough 57%

Hot Press 28%

11%

57%

32%

11%

Artboard Usage in 2012
Showing the importance of our illustrations
Segment Area: Percent of Expenses • Segment Height: Percent of Sales

Ebook graphic solutions

It might seem as if the low-resolution (72 dpi) monitor graphics of the Web are a clear place for bitmap graphics. However, even here the creative freedom and flexibility of vector graphics give you a decided speed and efficiency

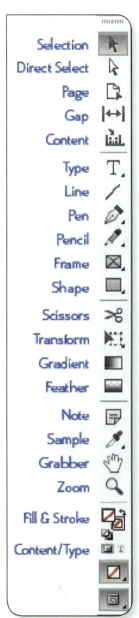

Selection
Direct Select
Page
Gap
Content

Type
Line
Pen
Pencil
Frame
Shape

Scissors
Transform
Gradient
Feather

Note
Sample
Grabber
Zoom

Fill & Stroke

Content/Type

advantage over people who are limited to Photoshop or less when it comes to graphic creation for online use. Bitmaps are very difficult to edit [often impossible] unless everything is in it's own layer.

Bitmap painting programs are extremely clumsy for quick, clear graphic production. PDF graphics from InDesign can easily be rasterized as GIFs, PNGs, or JPEGs at any size, resolution, or color space you need. By using color PDFs that can quickly be rasterized to the exact size needed, you obtain a design freedom and image control that are very difficult to accomplish in Photoshop.

The first time you try to make type fit a certain size, transform it, or simply scale type in Photoshop, you will long for the freedom of InDesign. Modified type in an InDesign PDF rasterizes clearly and sharply when compared to transformed type done in Photoshop

The tools available

InDesign does have most of the relevant Illustrator tools: but they are laid out in a way that is instantly recognizable as page layout. Strange tools like the graphing tool, gradient mesh, blending tool, and so forth are missing, as they should be. This is a page layout program. This is not primarily a graphics creation program—vector or bitmap. Yet, the basic drawing tools are all here.

The toolbox looks comfortingly familiar. If you are used to Illustrator it seems streamlined and clean. The dizzying cacophony of dozens of tools on pop out menus from the toolbox are largely missing.

What tools are left are the path manipulation tools—and they are really all you need. If you need a fancy 3D drawing with realistic shadows, you belong in Illustrator. If you needrealistic textures you need to go to Photoshop. But my guess is that InDesign will be all you need much of the time.

You've been using several of these tools throughout the book already. But once you start drawing with them, their usage changes and I need to be sure you know their capabilities.

The Selection tools

The Selection [V] and Direct Selection [A] tools are very similar to Illustrator's in appearance. The hollow pointed or white arrow does path editing. If you need to move a frame or resize it, you need the Selection tool. If you want to modify the shape in any way, you need the Direct Selection capabilities. You also have to go to one of the selection tools to modify the wrap on the text frames. The Selection tool also includes the Rotation tool.

TIP: One of the disconcerting aspects of this new page layout setup is the simple fact that you can have two separate text wraps on the same object. One for the selected frame, and another for the selected frame content. Don't confuse yourself. Be careful.

The Pen Tool [P]

InDesign's Pen tool is very definitely Illustrator's four part Pen tool: with all of its advantages and disadvantages. I have found that InDesign's version works the way that I wish Illustrator's or Photoshop's did.

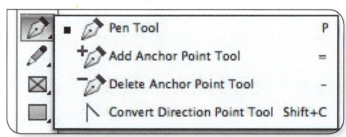

For those of you who are not familiar with Adobe's pen tool, it makes paths by clicking [placing a corner point] and clock-dragging [placing a smooth point] in a connect-the-dots fashion (more on that in a bit).

You have to closely watch the tool when producing or editing a path to find out what is happening. If you see a little plus next to the tool (over an existing path), clicking will add a point. If you see a little minus, clicking will subtract one. If you see the little open pointer, clicking will change the point type from smooth to corner or vice versa. The shortcuts are the same as Illustrator's.

The basic advice is to remember that holding down the Command (Control) key changes you back to the last selection tool you used. Holding down the Option (Alt) key switches you to the Convert Point tool. The most disconcerting aspect is that there is no way to drag out handles on a corner point. All you can do is drag out the handles with the Change Point tool creating a curve point. Then move the Change Point tool over the handles that result. This allows you to drag the handles individually converting the curve point to a corner point with visible handles. InDesign's implementation seems very elegant and obvious.

Using The Pen Tool

The Pen tool is the core of PostScript illustration: This tool started with Fontographer 1986. This is the exact same tool Photoshop and Illustrator use for drawing paths. What I am trying to say is simple: "You must become fluent with the Pen tool!" This is not an option.

How do you add that skill? This is a very strange tool that does not seem intuitive at all: There is nothing like it anywhere else except in PostScript drawing programs. So let's talk a little about how you gain skill. I found this out when I went to the University of Minnesota in the late '60s to learn to be an artist.

When I went to the orientation session of my first drawing class, the final thing the professor said as we left (planning on coming back on Monday morning to have him "teach" us to draw) was, "Oh, by the way—when you come

Monday, bring sixty drawings that you have done over the weekend. I don't care what you draw, but you must bring sixty new drawings done in the next three days."

During that first nine-week course, we all drew nearly 600 drawings in pencil, conté crayon, charcoal, crowquill, and heavy bamboo dip pen. The first ones were horrible and I threw them away. I wish I had them now. All I'd have to do is look at them to realize I've gotten a little better, at least. The first year was all quantity over quality.

I didn't produce my first "keepers" until my second year, after four drawing courses, two painting courses, three courses on color theory, and so forth. By that time I had produced thousands of drawings, hundreds of stupid exercises, and more than twenty large paintings. They were starting to get fairly good—surprise, surprise!

You will have to do the same thing with the Pen tool. You just need to draw. Your real assignment, for the next few months, is to draw at least two dozen simple drawings a week, or more, with the Pen tool. In reality, I hope you will do many more than that. By the time you finish, you will be getting pretty good with the Pen tool.

How do you draw with paths?

You use various tools to place points. The points are placed in order around a shape & the path is produced by connecting them. These points are controlled by mathematical formulas to produce a path that can bend and change direc-

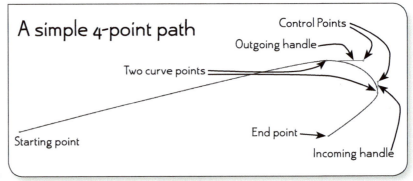

A simple 4-point path

Control Points
Outgoing handle
Two curve points
Starting point
End point
Incoming handle

tion under direct control. These modifications are determined by point location & handles with control points. Each point has two handles.

All shapes need to be drawn as one continuous outline or path. Drawing short lines and connecting them is an exercise in futility.

Corner points, Curve points, & Handles

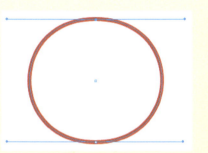

The 2-point circle
A deceptively simple project
Using your Pen Tool: Click-drag sideways, holding down the Shift Key [until the two handles look like what you see at the top of the circle]. Then release, hold-down the shift key again and click-drag below the top point in the other direction dragging the handles until they match the top handles. Then click-drag again on top of the top point, dragging to the left until your smart guides show things are lined up. I have a 3 pt red stroke on my circle.

The following descriptions and definitions are almost certainly not accurate mathematically. Who cares? What is important is that they will help you understand how your paths work so you can control them.

Points: These are the dots you place so that when you connect the dots a path is produced. A path has a direction going from the first point to the second point and so on. Our outside paths are drawn counterclockwise.

Path segments: A segment [for our purposes] is a portion of a path between two points. That's the old Fontographer/FreeHand definition and it works to let you know what is going on with your paths. So, a segment is a straight line from point to point plus any length added by handles at the beginning or the end.

Point Handles: These are tangent lines coming out of the points. A tangent is the straight line touching a curve at only that point without crossing the path.

Every segment has two handles: the outgoing handle from the point at the incoming end and an incoming handle from the point at the outgoing end. If a point appears to have no handles, or only a handle on one side of the point, the other handles simply have zero length. Zero length handles produce the shortest possible segment. If both the outgoing and incoming handles of a segment have zero length, you have the shortest possible segment: a straight line from point to point.

Handle Control Points: At the end of every handle is a small ball, x, square, or knob (depends on the app used) that can be grabbed with the mouse and moved to control the length & direction of the handle coming out of the point.

Corner points: When these are produced by a click of the Pen tool, they have no handles—actually, no handles are visible. In fact, they have handles with no length. What that means is that paths coming into that point or going out from that point will go the shortest way possible—modified by the handle at the other end of the segment. If a corner point has visible handles, each of them can be moved independently.

Smooth or Curve points: When these are produced with a click-drag, they have handles of equal length that are locked onto a common tangent. This means if you move one handle, the other handle moves in an equal but opposite direction. If the curve handles have been modified in length they rotate around the point in a single line in opposite directions while maintaining the length of the handles involved.

So, how does the Pen tool work?

So, with that intro, how does the tool work? When you simply click with the Pen, you produce corner points having no handles. When you click and then immediately drag, while still holding down the button, a curve point is produced. You drag out the outgoing handle which produces an equal incoming handle on the other side of the point on the same tangent as the handle you are dragging out. With these two options you can draw anything your little heart desires—easy, huh? Actually, it is that easy. Once you get accustomed to the tool, you will be amazed with its precision, dazzled by its fluidity, and addicted to its editable flexibility. It makes vector lines and shapes.

Constraining the tool: When clicking to produce corner points, holding down the Shift key will keep the points lined up on horizontal, vertical, or 45° angles. When click-dragging to produce a curve point, holding down the Shift key will cause the handles to be on horizontal, vertical, or 45° angles.

 Choose the Direct Selection tool first: before you start drawing with the Pen tool. Holding down the Command key while you are drawing gives you the last selection tool you used. This needs to be the Direct Selection tool because you will be editing the path and need access to the points and handles of that path.

While drawing in InDesign, you will constantly want to go to the Direct Selection tool to modify the point or points you just placed. This is normal. You should learn to resist that tendency, however. It is usually better to draw the entire path around the shape you are working on and close it by clicking on your starting point before you begin editing the path to perfect the shape.

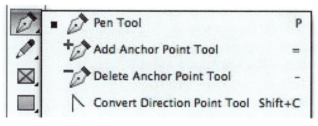

The Pen tool has four variations that appear automatically, or by holding down a modifier key

Type P to select the Pen tool: Draw path by clicking or click-dragging to produce the points you want. To repeat, draw a single continuous path around the entire object being drawn.

When you go to editing the path:

The Pen Icon will show you what is happening.

- **A plus appears (the Add Anchor Point tool):** When the Pen is held over an empty portion of a segment—clicking will add a point.

- **A minus appears (the Delete Anchor Point tool):** If the tool is held over an existing point—clicking will delete that point.

- **If the tool is held over a point with the Option key held down (the Convert Direction Point tool):** clicking will convert that point from a corner to a curve (and you can drag out the handles) or it will convert from a curve to a corner point and the handles will disappear (go to zero length).

- **If the tool is held over a handle control point of a curve point with the Option key held down (accessing the Convert Direction Point tool):** the curve point will be converted to a corner point (without contracting the handles) and the handle can be dragged independently.

As you are drawing, if you do not like the way the handles are arranged, or the shape of a segment, simply press down the Command key (PC: Control) to access the last Selection tool used. Click on a point to select it and the handles will appear for that point (the outgoing handle of the preceding point, both handles of the selected point, and the incoming handle of the following point). Adjust the point location and the handles as you decide they need to be set, then release the Command key to go back to the Pen tool, click on the end point to select it and continue drawing the path.

 Very important tip: Every shape must be drawn in one continuous path. If you need a closed path, you have to draw in one continuous path the entire way around the shape. If you find you have two or more parts to your path, delete all except the first one, click on the end point to select it, and redraw it as one continuous path. This is the most common mistake of beginning Pen users. Yes, parts can be joined together, but it is frustrating, clumsy, and slow to execute. Don't do it! Bad Habit!

Frame generators

The next three tools are a little confusing, because Adobe has made them two separate menus: the frame tools and the shape tools. Frames have no fill or stroke. But with the x running from corner to corner, you can select and move them easily even though they are empty. Shape tools use the currently selected fill and stroke. But, it doesn't make any difference which one you are using. If you have a shape and click in it with the Type tool, it becomes a text frame. If you have a text frame with no type or insertion point in it, into which you place a graphic—it becomes a graphic frame. Graphics placed into a text frame insertion point become inline graphics.

The Frame Tools

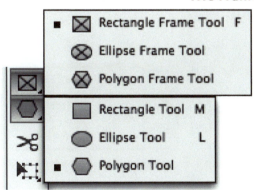

The Frame tools have no stroke or fill, yet you can move them around by clicking anywhere within the frame [they have a non-printing x though them]. The shape tools (Rectangle, Ellipse, and Polygon) can only be selected by clicking on the stroke unless you have a fill assigned to the shape.

The Rectangle Tool [M] & the Ellipse Tool [L]

These tool are the normal drawing tools. If you hold down the Shift key; the shape is constrained to a square or circle. If you hold down the Option (Alt) key, they draw from the center out. They also draw from handle to handle like any shape tools.

The Polygon Tool

This tool is the normal limited version of the Polygon tool available from Adobe products. As you can see from the dialog capture below, the shape of the points of the star must be guessed. There is no preview. With an infinite variety of stars possible with every number of points, this makes this tool useless except for drawing frames for regular polygons (hence the name, I guess). Or I guess if you really want a star, you can do and redo until you get something usable.

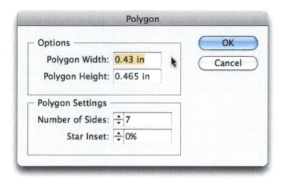

Shape generators produce closed paths

These paths can be edited like any other path with the Direct Selection tool and the Pen Tool. In addition you can modify these shapes with the Corner Options. As you can clearly see on the opposite page, you can quickly get ridiculous with it all. But the controls are easy to use and very quick to execute. Once you have what you want you can leave it selected and make a new Object style which will save all your setting into a style.

The Pencil tool

This is a typical Illustrator triple tool: Pencil, Smoother, and Eraser. The Pencil draws freehand paths with no point control. The Smoother progressively smooths out the line (without any real control, although it often does a nice job). You can access the Smoother tool by holding down the Option key while you draw. The Eraser does what you would like it to, most of the time. It must be hand selected.

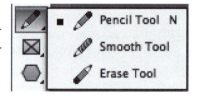

A really nice capability is that the Smoother and Eraser work on any path you draw, with any tool. The Smoother, for example, will convert a star into a polygon with concave sides (it changes the entire shape). They even work on type converted to paths, but the effects are rather unpredictable. In general, however, these are a very elegant selection of freehand drawing tools. The main issue is the lack of control

Click-drag here to anchor object

Click here to modify corners

Once clicked the corners look like this. Dragging on the diamond modifies all 4 corners. Option-clicking on the corners will switch them between the six types: None, Rounded, Inverse Rounded, Inverse Corner, Bevel, & Fancy. Shift-clicking will enable you to modify a corner individually. The corner options dialog will help you control and keep track of what you've done.

Then you can color and shape it however you like.

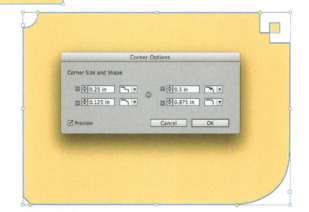

Corner Options

Corner Size and Shape:

0.25 in   0.5 in

0.125 in   0.875 in

☑ Preview   Cancel   OK

Below is with a Thick-Thin-Thick 7-pt Blue stroke with a light blue Gap, and a radial fill

over point type or placement. I can't remember the last time I used the Pencil tool.

Converting shapes

This capability is only found at the bottom of the Object menu when you have an object selected. You can convert any shape (with corner modifications or not) into a Rectangle, Rounded Rectangle, Beveled Rectangle, Inverse Rounded Rectangle, Ellipse, Triangle, Polygon, Line, or Orthogonal Line. It works very well.

Corner Options

This is shown on the previous page: sorry 'bout that.

Drawing in InDesign is obviously limited

However, even with these limitations in InDesign, the transformation tools are all available as are the Photoshop effects. You'll be surprised how often InDesign's tool set is more than enough. If you are creating a drawing or painting you will either be using fine art media or using Illustrator or Photoshop. Paint and FreeHand work well also, but you'll have a little trouble converting them to a format you can use in InDesign.

The main new skill you'll need is the pen tool: you'll need to practice

Combining paths

Now that we understand points, segments, handles, and paths, we need to discuss methods of using multiple paths to produce discrete objects. This is often done best with the Layers palette. On a regular basis, graphic production is greatly enhanced by having the separate objects of our illustrations on separate layers that can be turned on and off as needed.

 TIP: Don't add a layer unless you have a good reason. A layer should be added to help you organize, not to add unnecessary complexity. Many of my students quickly got lost in a morass of layers that were not only unnecessary, but served only to confuse the designer. If you need a layer, create one. Simply refuse to add a layer unless you have a specific need and a logical reason for that additional layer of information.

However, this section covers those groups of paths that you need to keep in a permanent relationship for various reasons. Sometimes layers will help you sort things out, but that is not what we are talking about here—at all. That type of layer usage is a Photoshop thing. Now we are talking about capabilities that put InDesign and PostScript Illustration far above all other graphic software.

There are basically three ways to combine paths: grouping, making a composite path, and (for now, let's call it) merging. They all have their uses, and it is important to understand their differences in concept. Almost everyone understands and uses grouping. It is probably the most overused capability of digital publishing software. The most common question I was asked by my students was,

"Why won't this work?" (Usually with a whining twist.) The first thing I usually had to do was Ungroup several times to get to a place where I could show them how to fix what they were trying to do.

Grouping

DEFINITION: Grouping is the establishment of a permanent relationship between multiple objects, without changing any of those objects in any way. There is no interaction between the objects

If I group a man's hat with his head, whenever I move his head, his hat moves also. There are a couple of things to remember about grouping. As simple as it is, many think that grouping is the best way to protect yourself from accidental changes. There are some problems with that. They primarily involve changes that make normal workflow more difficult. If you get into the habit of always ungrouping as soon as you are done transforming the group, it will help you in the long run as you work with your graphic.

Please notice that any transformation of the group transforms every piece of the group while maintaining the original relationships. All of the fills remain the same. None of the paths are altered in any way. However, the strokes will vary in thickness as you scale up or down. As a result, there is very little use for grouping other than to gather various paths into a temporary unit to enable transformation as a single piece. Even here you need to be careful.

TIP: Grouping adds memory requirements when printing. So, in general, you should always remember to ungroup after grouping for a temporary purpose. It will solve some printing problems. As usual, be conscious of your actions.

Our other methods of combining paths actually change the paths in some manner.

Let us look at the method that changes the fills.

Composite paths [joining]

An old name for composite paths [joining] is good, for in a real way the paths used are joined into one path. However, it is a very special type of joining. First of all, it has several rules, which we will cover next. Second, it fundamentally changes the appearance of the paths by giving them a single overall fill and stroke.

The rules of joining

1. **All paths to be composited must be ungrouped:** When type is converted to Outlines, the entire text block becomes a group. When ungrouped, often each line of type remains a group. When each line is ungrouped, you finally have access to the individual paths (except for characters that are composited). With composited characters, you must use Object>> Path>> Release Composited Path.
2. **All paths must be closed paths.**

When the two rules are satisfied, all the paths to be joined are selected and then composited. When paths are composited, some very special effects appear. First of all, the new composite path has a single stroke and fill, based on the path farthest back in the layering of the paths.

Even/Odd Fill

The second, and probably most important, attribute of composite paths is that they should have an even/odd fill. This is where the single fill appears and disappears as it passes through the various sections of the composite path. Here again it is probably easier to show you with type characters, because the most common composite paths are letters.

The only problem is that Adobe doesn't do this very well. You will often find that it is easier to take the interior paths and make sure they are on top. Then go to the Pathfinder panel and use Subtract. This will take the top path and punch a hole in the path behind it.

The most useful part of this even/odd fill is that the unfilled portions are not white — they are transparent, empty, open areas within the composite path. When you think about this, these transparent areas are essential for almost every graphic design. This is why Photoshop is essential, it offers bitmapped transparency. But vector is better.

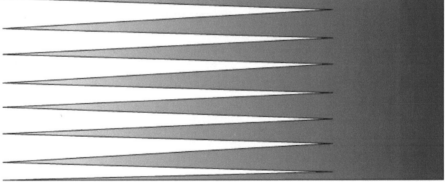

How would we deal with letters like O, P, R, a, b, d, and so on, if the counters were not transparent? Every time we placed type over a colored background, we would have to manually select the paths of the counters and color them the color of the background. This can be done. But what happens when you want to place type over a photograph or a gradient fill? It is impossible to match portions taken from the middle of a gradient. Type is filled with composite paths to solve this problem.

Of course, this even/odd fill attribute of composite paths can get a bit out of hand. Below, you can see that the word FAST is fairly chewed up. I had to try several fonts for that word before it was legible. As you can see, it is important to look at these joined paths carefully to make sure that readability has not been compromised. [By the way, the illustration below was done in InDesign because I could not get it to work in Illustrator].

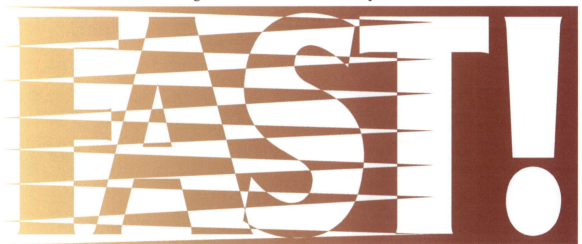

Pathfinder filters

There are several path-combining filters that you will use regularly. These path-combining capabilities, found in the Pathfinder panel, enable you to combine paths in ways that will greatly enhance your drawing production speed.

Pathfinder Panel

This panel hold many commands to modify and convert paths. Simply select the shapes and click the button. As you can see, there are four basic choices: Paths, PathFinder, Convert Shape, and Convert Point.

Pathfinder Panel

Paths
Join, Open, Close, Reverse Direction

Pathfinder
Add, Subtract, Intersect, Exclude, Minus

Convert Shape
Rectangle, Rounded, Bevel, Inverted, Ellipse
Triangle, Polygon, Line, Vertical or Horizontal

Convert Point
Plain, Corner, Smooth, Symmetrical

Paths

These are very important options that are not really available in Illustrator [though they need to be there].

- **Join:** Connects two endpoints
- **Open:** Opens a closed path
- **Close:** Closes an open path
- **Reverse Path:** Changes the direction of the path

Of these for path operations, the last one is critical. This is the one that Illustrator needs but does not have. It is used because, as mentioned, Adobe does not do even / odd fill on its compound paths very well. Compound paths are produced in PostScript by having the path directions reversed. If the inside path is reversed in direction when compared to the outside path, it will punch a hole in the outside path. You see the results of that with the FAST! Graphic on the previous page.

However, this is easier to do with Pathfinder by using the Subtract operation.

Pathfinder Operations

I started with these three shapes: As I go through these operations, it is important to observe the layering of the shapes and the fills applied to each. Normally the attributes of the top shape will apply. This is a 1-point Black stroke with a 41%-0% gradient fill. Path combination operations in both applications often result in a composite path. Obviously, this is part of the strangeness of working with a collage of shapes — the uniqueness of PostScript illustration.

Start with Add

I've always known this as Unite, which was the old name for it in FreeHand. What it does is obvious. It takes all the selected shapes and makes a new shape which goes around the outside of all the shapes. As you can see it uses the attribute of the top shape.

Next we'll use Subtract

Here we see that the top two shapes were each punched out of the back shape. The attributes of the back shape were retained: 1-point Black stroke with a 12%–77% gradient fill.

Now we'll do Intersect

This gives us the small rectangle where the three shapes all overlap. It has the attributes of the top shape.

Now for Exclude Overlap

This is very interesting. We get a compound path of the three shapes. It uses the attributes of the top shape. Most interesting to me is the fact that this exhibits perfect even/odd fill. That is very rare for Adobe, and far superior to Illustrator.

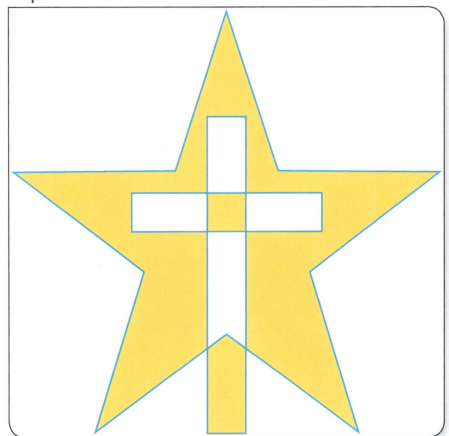

Finally let's see Minus Back

This one is also interesting. Subtracting the star from the top two shapes eliminated the horizontal reactangle, but left a blunt arrow from the bottom rectangle. But

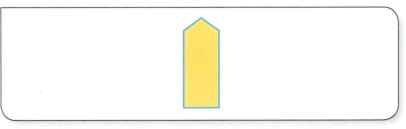

notice the fill. It is the fill of the top shape, but its width is the same as the star so with a gradient we would get the center portion of the gradient showing in the blunt arrow.

As you can see from the preceding examples, these are handy tools. As a practical matter making compound paths, I normally put the shape I want to punch out of the bottom shape on top, select both and use Subtract or Exclude Overlap. I used to use reverse path direction as recently as CS5, but now the path operations work the way I want them to.

Paste Inside

Here we have one of those commonly used capabilities that is trouble from the start. The idea is to take a shape and fill it with a photo or illustration. One of the reasons Paste Inside is used so often is that it is so easy to understand. It seems to be a simple — and very powerful — cropping tool. In fact, it does not crop at all. It provides a boundary where the images pasted inside are revealed inside the path and not seen outside the path. However (like all clipping paths), the portions of the images that seem to be cropped are merely hidden. All you did was add data telling the printer not to print those areas outside the clipping path. To translate, this means you have added a lot of file size.

The problem with Paste Into is the final result: Aside from the complexity and the possible printing problems, the same question has to be asked, "Does this help communicate clearly with the reader?" In most cases, the answer is a clear, "No!" I am not saying to avoid these options. I am repeating that you really need to keep your priorities straight and work carefully.

To adjust the image inside the paths: With the Selection tool, simply click on the content donut and move the masked image around as needed. If you move it so that it no longer fills the entire interior of the paths, then the original fill color will show [in this cases, the bright red fill used for the word WARNING!].

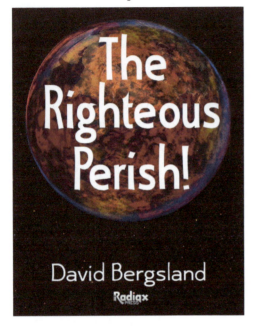

WARNING!

I started with this book cover and the word WARNING! I selected the word and used Type>> Create Outlines to covert it to paths. Then I moved the image on top of the type and Cut it. Then I selected the type and chose Edit>> Paste Into. As you can see the bitmapped image is masked by the shapes of the letters. As you can also see the result is a mess. Neither the word nor the Title on the book cover can be read without a lot of effort.

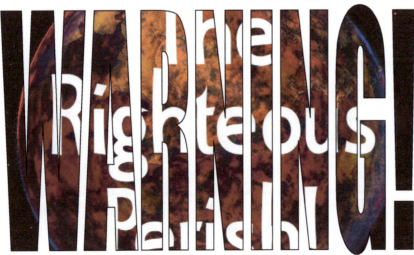

These path combination tools are simply part of your arsenal. You will find most of them invaluable as you run into the deadlines of real-world employment. It's a real shock to many graduates to discover that most graphics are not budgeted — meaning they have to be done very fast. It is not at all unusual to be forced to generate a competent graphic in twenty minutes or less. The power of PostScript illustration, with its ability to freely combine, edit, and manipulate paths, enables this to be a realistic and very common requirement.

Create outlines [manipulating type]

On the opposite page, I casually mentioned one of InDesign's most powerful tools: converting type to editable paths. There are many reasons why you might want to do this. But first, what does this command do? It converts type characters to editable PostScript paths.

These shapes are no longer editable type

There are many times when this is required. One of the most common is the Paste Into scenario we looked at on the opposite page. But it is also used to produce logos and graphics for your books. Book titles on book covers are commonly edited by selecting the title and executing the Create Outlines command in the Type Menu. Then the resulting paths are modified to produce a distinctive title.

I don't think I mentioned it back when I showed you this graphic, but the word FAST had to be converted to paths before I could punch it out of the multi-pointed rectangle.

The word Radiqx in the publishing house logo had to be converted to outlines so I could modify the R and then subtract the cross shape. In fact, those font outlines are already there in the font—used to produce the font, but the Create Outlines command gives us access to them so that they can be edited and manipulated.

Eliminating the need for a font

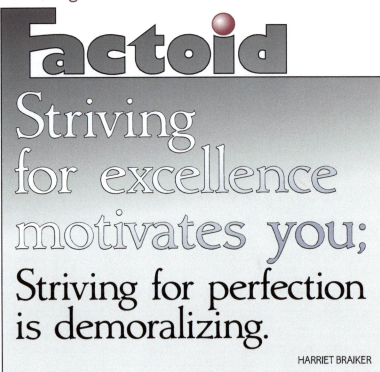

Striving for excellence motivates you; Striving for perfection is demoralizing.

HARRIET BRAIKER

This is what the word looked like: before I converted it to paths so I could make the frame to hold the quote. It is set in Gill Sans Ultra Bold—one of the free fonts which

comes with the MacOS. All I did was make the F a bit larger, drag the stem down, add a couple points with the Pen tool, and dragged them sideways to make the rectangle. Of course I had to modify the a so I could unite it with the F, and then move the counter of the a on top and punch it out of the Fa shape. The quote is just set on top of the new rectangle and colored as live type (try that with Photoshop). I forgot! I had to cut and paste back the dot over the i so I could enlarge it, center it, and color it with a radial gradient.

I did it all in a new InDesign document, 6"x6", exported it as a PDF and placed it into the copy on the opposite page. When it comes to do the ebooks, I'll open the PDF into Photoshop, rasterizing it to 600 pixels wide. I'll then save it as a PSD, and Save For Web to get a tiny little JPEG that will work fine in the ePUB and KF8 versions.

Typographic graphics

Making a quick graphic in InDesign is a common occurrence. It is something a word processor cannot do. If you need your images even fancier, you can take your typographic beginnings and finish them off in Photoshop.

Linking graphics

This is one of the most common issues when people begin building their books in InDesign. Many people add graphics by copy/pasting. Worse yet, many want to embed their graphics. Basically, you "never" want to do either of these things. **Embedding bloats file size:** This book, for example, has 69.7 MB of graphics at this point in the design of the print version [229 graphics listed so far]. If I embedded the graphics, InDesign would crash. It cannot use enough RAM to keep things going [as if I could afford enough anyway or find a machine which can hold a twenty gigabytes of RAM]. **Copy/Paste and/or embedding make updating almost impossible:** If I make any changes to a graphic outside of InDesign,

I have to re-paste or re-embed to add those changes to my document. This goes far beyond tedious.

This is one major advantage to InDesign

What we need is a way to add the graphics that keeps them outside the document with a method of updating changed graphics that is simple and easy. This has always been one of the main strengths of professional page layout software. I put all my graphics in a folder called Links inside the folder containing my InDesign document. If I do not move them there first, I move them as I add them.

Links panel

This is actually one of InDesign's strong points. No one does it better. As you can see above, not only can you link to graphics with only a placeholder appearing in the actual document, but, you can also easily update any changes. You can relink to a different version [B&W to Color, for example] or a completely different graphic. You can click a button to show the graphic in its actual location. And much more.

Status:

This column has two icons. These both cause major problems if they are not fixed. If either of these icons appear, all that will print is the low-resolution screen image which InDesign has created to show you the graphic in InDesign.

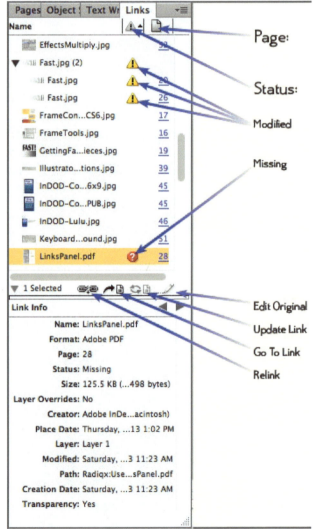

Missing: This red stop sign means that the link to the graphic has been broken. It may be deleted, it may be on a different hard drive, it or a containing folder may have been renamed. Whatever the problem is, it won't print or show up in your ebook. You need to find the graphic and link it again. You use the Relink button below.

Modified: This Yellow triangle means that the placed graphic has been changed or modified in some way. You need to click on Update Link to fix the problem.

Page:

This shows you the location of placed graphic. If you click on a link in this column InDesign will take you to the graphic on that page.

PB: Pasteboard: This means the graphic linked is placed on the pasteboard somewhere [it's not on a page]. You must click on the link to see what the problem is and fix it. Items on the pasteboard will not print, nor will they show up in your ebooks, but they regularly cause serious printing problems and ebooks problems as the printer or ereader goes looking for the non-existent graphic.

Button Bar:

Relink: This enables you to relink to any graphic you have available on your hard drive or server. I'll use this to find and link the graphic which is shown as missing.

Find Link: This will change the page view, centering the graphic on the page where it is used. For example, you can see in the capture that the selected PSD is on the pasteboard somewhere. I need to go there and fix that.

Update link: Sometimes this is updated automatically. Sometimes you actually need to click on this button. You can tell which is needed by the Yellow Triangle found in the second column from the right.

Edit graphic [Edit Original]: This tries to open the original graphic and works well if you have a Photoshop graphic or an AI file. In fact, it not only opens the original graphic, but when you save it, InDesign automatically updates it. However, for PDFs it does not go to the original but tries to open the PDF instead (which is a pain).

Ah well, you can't have everything. Of course, it doesn't help at all if the original is an RGB full resolution graphic stored in originals. All my greyscale images in this book have a full color, full resolution version from which they were saved stored in the Originals folder. Also, it doesn't work when the original is a PSD, from which you Saved for Web a PNG, JPEG, or GIF for your ePUB or KF8 book.

Copy link to folder

If you place a graphic which is not located in the links folder, you can simply right-click on it in the Links panel. This will give you the command seen to the right: Copy Link(s) To... Once you choose your Links folder a copy will be placed there and the link updated.

Must you use a links folder? No: But, You can actually know where all your graphics are located, when it is time for you to make your Color PDF, ePUB, and Kindle KF8 versions. If you have all the graphics in a Links folder, and all the full color

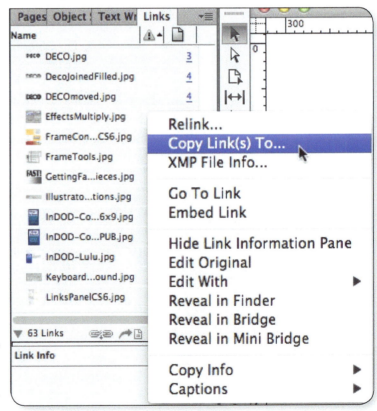

originals in the Originals folder, file management becomes much easier.

Why have a full color originals folder?

That is simple. When I go to make the color version for the color PDFs, all I have to do is drop the color images into the Links folder. All the greyscale images are replaced by the color originals (they both have identical names). Simply updating does a lot of my preparation work for the downloadable color PDFs I sell through Scribd and Lulu.

When I do my ePUBs

All I have to do is save my color RGB PSDs into JPEGs. They must be resampled to the proper size and then saved into a new Links folder in the new ePUB document folder. Then relinking is relatively easy for that conversion also (though it is not automated) because the name has changed.

The Swatches Panel

There is no program which handles color as well as InDesign—not even close.

Even though Illustrator has a Swatches panel, it is very difficult and clumsy to set up a custom palette for your book. InDesign makes it easy. InDesign swatches work very much like styles. They have the same global control as a style does. If you double-click to open the Swatch Options dialog box. You can modify your swatch as much as you like. When you close the dialog every instance of that color [including those used as color stops for gradients will be updated throughout the book. If you import a color, you can delete it and replace it with the colors used in your book palette.

A designed palette of swatches

One of the things that trips up most designers when they start using styles is the fact that styles can only use colors that are already set up as swatches. This may seem like another hassle, but in fact it is a blessing in disguise. This situation forces you to set up a designed set of swatches.

Why would you want a special color palette?: That is obvious once you think about it. Your color choices are as much a core part of your personal style as the typography & layout choices. We all have a constantly evolving set of colors we use. For most of us (at least at the beginning) these color choices change with fashion. For many of us, these fashion choices remain a key part of our evolving design sense.

What is clear is the factory defaults are ugly ◇◇◇◇◇◇◇

CMY & RGB are building blocks of color. CMYK is printing color. RGB is monitor color. As self publishing using on-demand printing we work in RGB almost exclusively. The six default colors are not to be used alone except in those rare instances where magenta is actually a stylistic statement you want to make. It makes no difference if you like pastels or jewel tones; bold, saturated hues or subtle shades of color. The only universal constant is that no one except the laziest designers uses CMYRGorB. My experience is that we all need the six basic hues (red, orange, yellow, green, blue, & violet), some selected tints of those hues, plus a few gradients. All of these things are necessary for use in developing a gorgeous, truly useful set of styles. Remember, if you do not have them in Swatches, you are going to have to constantly save your style temporarily to go back and make any swatches you need. Then you have to edit the style again to add the colors you just made.

Set up your color palette for all versions
before you design the first version ◇◇◇◇◇◇◇

Although it is true that your print version at Createspace and/or Lulu will be printed in greyscale, You will immediately need to change the color palette to RGB for your downloadable PDFs. You will use that color palette for all your ebooks. You will find that really helps to have your palette set up before you start adjusting your styles. It helps immensely to keep the look of the book consistent.

My Current Set of Swatches

To the left you can see what I am currently using in this book. It probably does not match what you like. But it is probably better than the defaults being currently used by you unless you've customized them. If your panel does not look like this you need to chose Name in the panel menu. We'll cover that menu in a bit.

Controlling the global look with different clients

Because all styles have this color palette embedded, when I begin work on a new book I merely have to modify the existing swatches to completely change the color styling of the piece. To replace a tint of the purple with one of the red, you simply make the new tint and then take the purple tint and delete it. This gives you the dialog that allows you to substitute the new tint for all the instances of the existing tint. Modifying a swatch changes all the tints of that swatch and all the gradients where it is used.

In this way, you can easily modify the custom palette to bring it in line: with the needs of your differing books and clients (if you are designing for others also). You can also

---

Swatches | Paragrap | **Effects**

Tint: 100 %

[None]	
[Registration]	
[Paper]	
[Black]	
R=179 G=28 B=33	
R=255 G=228 B=114	
R=37 G=64 B=143	
R=55 G=153 B=64	
[Black] 55%	
[Black] 41%	
[Black] 77%	
[Black] 12%	
[Black] 21%	
0-15	
0-21	
0-21 2	
12-77	
21-77Radial	
41-0	

automate the application of these colors with the designed set of styles we've covered.

 Controlling Gray tints: After telling you that you can easily delete a color and change all the resultant tints, I need to mention that you might find it helpful to make a NewBlack swatch and make your tints from that. This way you can easily change your grey tints for purple tints by deleting the NewBlack and replacing it with the purple you desire.

Reading the swatches

In order to understand what you are doing in InDesign when applying colors, you need to be able to read the icons used that tell you what type of color you are using.

In my earlier books, I had an entire chapter on color usage and Separations. There used to be major problems if you did not keep track of the color spaces you were using. For now, all the free self publishing suppliers use RGB. So, you will do good to do that yourself. Nevertheless, you need to be careful because not all color prints or views as you might expect. As you can see above, InDesign packs a lot of information into each bar. Aspects like the color space used to display the color, whether it is a spot color, tint, or a process color, and whether you can redefine the color. First of all, colors in [Brackets] cannot be redefined for output (although [Paper] and [Registration] can be redefined for viewing on the monitor).

Let's start with the top bar.

[None]: As you know, the crossbar in all cases (icon, tool, or swatch) is red. It is to clearly warn you that there is nothing there. It means what it says, None. As you know, we are dealing with PostScript. The PostScript descriptions have no color or dimension until we specify it — in InDesign's case, color is defined by clicking on a swatch including the specification of [None] (not transparent color but none).

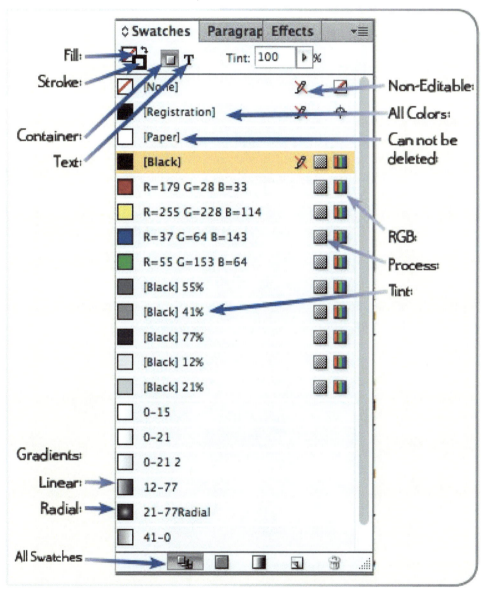

Notice: The pencil with the slash through it means that this color cannot be redefined [labeled non-editable].

[Paper]: This is not white, as you know, or is it? Under normal use, Paper is an opaque knockout color with no color that reveals the paper through the knocked out hole. In InDesign you can actually make the Paper color appear to be the color of the paper you will be using. Just double-click the Paper swatch and make the swatch look as close as you can to the color of the paper you will be using. Of course, you can not imitate fiber-added stock, and you have to be aware that it's still just that opaque knockout with which you are familiar once it prints.

[Black]: This, again, is one of those colors never thought about — but it really requires knowledge. First of all, this is process black. Even though it is often treated like a spot color, this is process black (think 70% gray). If you are working in CMYK, you will probably need to create a separate swatch called something like Rich Black. If you are printing it in spot color, remember to specify that the press operator use dense black if it is important. Notice the slashed pencil. This color is yet another that cannot be redefined. By default it always overprints. To the right of the swatch you see the four-sided box that tells you this a CMYK color.

[Registration]: This color prints on all plates and is used for registration marks that must print on all colors. You can change the color that registration colored objects appear on the screen.

[Black] 21%: Here we have a tint of Black. As you can see from the swatch, it is a 21% tint, process color, CMYK. The little gray square that shows us process color shows up for CMYK, RGB, and LAB color. The only way you can tell which model is being used for the color is to look at the second icon just to the right of the process icon.

The final six swatches are gradient swatches. You can tell the top five are linear gradations and the bottom one is a radial gradient. It is a bit frustrating to have to add the gradients to the swatches palette to get any real control over them, but you get used to it after a while.

Swatches Panel Menu

When you are setting up your color palette for your book, you use the three dialogs seen here at the top of the Swatches Panel Menu: New Color Swatch…, New Tint Swatch…, and New Gradient Swatch…. The Mixed Ink Swatch have no use to use in self publishing. They are used for spot color work, mixing tints and shades of two spot colors. They are very complex, and none of the on-demand printing presses can use spot color anyway. This is for extremely top-end commercial printing.

Save & Load Swatches

This gives you the ability to Save your custom swatches into a file which can be imported into any InDesign document where they are needed.

Add unnamed colors

This is not much of a problem for us any more, but colors used which are not named [and therefore showing in the Swatches panel], can cause bad printing problems with some companies. As long as you make all your swatches with the Add New… dialogs, this is not an issue.

List by name

Always use this one. If you do not, none of the icons we use to determine what type of color we are using are available. You can select a swatch within the panel and drag it up or down to arrange them for easy use. You don't have to do this, but sooner or later it will bite you if you don't.

Creating & Adjusting Swatches

The New Color Swatch dialog is where you start: Actually, you a truly better off if you start [before you've applied any color] by choosing Select All Unused in the panel menu and then delete. This will give you a basic panel with {None}, [Paper], [Registration], and [Black]. These are the four colors which cannot be deleted or changed. You can tell that by the fact that the color names are enclosed in brackets. [Paper] is editable in that you can adjust to be the color of your paper, but it prints white regardless. Plus, we do not really have paper choices as on-demand publishers.

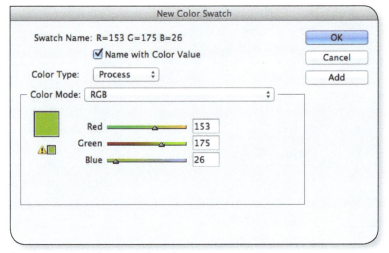

Swatch Name: I still use the color values for the name. You should learn how to recognize color by its color components. However, if you uncheck the box, you can name the color whatever you like: such as Dried Mustard or Competition Yellow.

Color Type: Here you have two choices: Process or Spot. Spot color is an important method of saving printing costs when printing traditionally. But on-demand printing always prints in Black & White or CMYK at this point. It cannot print RGB, because RGB is the color space of light not ink.

Color Mode: Our choices are CMYK or RGB. Technically, we should always use CMYK. But there are many problems here because CMYK is the color of ink and computer screens can only show color by blending the three RGB colors. There is a fairly radical color shift when converting RGB to CMYK.

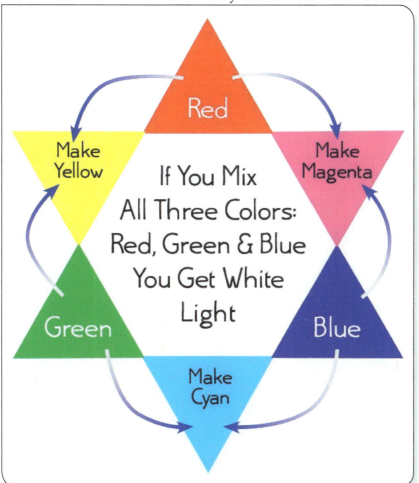

If You Mix All Three Colors: Red, Green & Blue You Get White Light

If you let Amazon or Lulu do it for you, there is no control of those color shifts. However, Createspace and Lulu both do better at matching what you see on your monitor if you send them RGB and let them convert the color for you.

 Building colors in RGB: You may have some difficulty building colors in RGB. Because this is the color space of light, it follows very different and polar opposite colors. In RGB, red plus green makes yellow; blue plus green makes cyan; and red plus blue makes magenta.

Thankfully, as you can see in the New Color Swatch dialog, the color sliders are colored so you can which way to go to mix the color you need.

The New Tint Swatch Dialog

This capability is very important: because you can not imagine how complex it is to attempt to make a 35% tint of R=20, G=101, B=38. If you're curious it is R=173; G=201; B=179 (remember more light gives lighter colors). But with the Tint Swatch dialog, it is very easy.

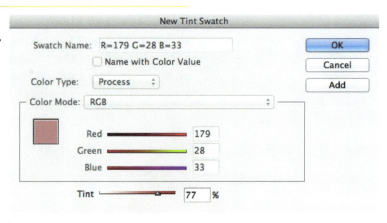

The New Gradient Swatch dialog

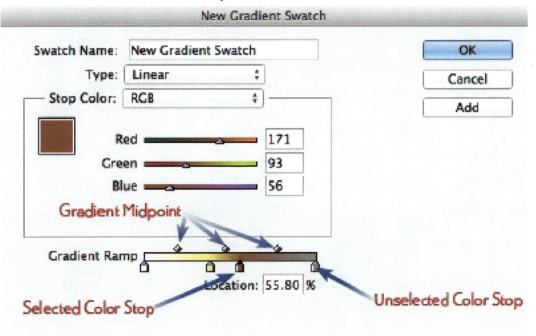

Gradients are really nice: I know I overuse them, but they give life to a page. The only real problem at this point is that

HTML/CSS gradients are not available to ePUBs or Kindle KF8 books. You can have as many stops as you can fit on that bar [I think I did forty once in an early book].

The Gradient panel [not shown]

As mentioned, this palette is much tougher to use than the dialog box that comes up when you use the New Gradient Swatch command on the Swatches Panel Options menu. It's confusing to add the colors because there is no specification for them. There is a reverse direction button that has been added. But they are not named, They are not in the Swatches panel, so you cannot use them in any of the various styles you will be using. It's a waste of time and you do not want to use it.

The Color panel [not shown]

This one, also, should be forgotten. The New Color Swatch command is far more powerful and intuitive. This panel changes the color of whichever is active: stroke or fill. It does not add the color to the Swatches palette. Having unspecified colors roaming around your document is asking for disaster. Do not ever use colors in your documents except from the Swatches palette!

How & why to produce your graphics

Start everything in RGB color

Because PDF, ePUB, and Kindle have no penalty for color, you need to start there. You can always make a greyscale version for print, if necessary. However, if you start with greyscale, colorizing the images is often nearly impossible. If you are printing in color, most on-demand suppliers do better with an RGB image anyway. Those who require a CMYK image merely force you to make a color adjustment in Photoshop.

Start your Photoshop files in high resolution ◇◇◇◇◇◇◇◇

Not only do you want color (where possible), but you also want the highest resolution you will ever need in any of your printed books or marketing pieces. Your modern ebooks (ePUBs and KF8) only support 72 dpi Web graphics at this point. But they need to be 600 pixels wide, at least. For the iPad, something like 1200 pixels wide would be excellent—but I can rarely use the resultant large book file sizes & KF8 has a 127K per image maximum.

Keep images in vector ◇◇◇◇◇◇◇◇◇

We've covered what a vector image is. Because of all the different variations you will need for the various formats, you will do better to use vector illustrations as much as possible. These can be AIs (Illustrator files), PDFs (from InDesign or Illustrator), or EPSs (from FreeHand or Illustrator). However, you need to make sure you keep track of the original documents to allow for changes as necessary. None of the final vector images are editable except for .ai files.

Why vector?

It's the most adjustable: Because vector files can be resized with no problems and rasterized at any size or resolution you need, you can have one graphic master file for all your needs in the various formats. It is also much easier to change color spaces with vector images—especially if you are using InDesign for your drawings. The Swatches panel in InDesign makes conversions like this very easy— as long as you have sense enough to have a predefined color palette.

Let me cover some of the possibilities. InDesign works very well with Illustrator, for example. Of course, you can drop in native Illustrator (.ai) files. Because of the Links panel this is the best idea for AI files. What you may not realize is that you can bring in editable paths from AI. All it takes is a little set up to the application preferences.

In Illustrator you need to go to preferences ◇◇◇◇◇◇◇

In preferences you must set up the Clipboard options. If you have PDF or transparency options set up anything you copy and paste from Illustrator will come in as a non-editable object. However, if you uncheck PDF and check the option which says AICB [no transparency support] and check the button which says preserve paths, you can then copy and paste editable paths into InDesign.

Dictionary & Hyphenation
Plug-ins & Scratch Disks
User Interface
File Handling & Clipboard
Appearance of Black

Clipboard on Quit
Copy As: ☐ PDF
☑ AICB (no transparency support)
◉ Preserve Paths
○ Preserve Appearance and Overprints

The art on the next page is an ellipse painted by a brushstroke from Illustrator. Let's give you a condensed description of the basic procedure:

- ❧ **In Illustrator, first I made a circle:** I chose the Ellipse tool and held down the shift key;

- ❧ **Picked a brushstroke and applied it:** These are found in the Brushes panel in AI;

- ❧ **Expanded its appearance (under the Object menu):** If I do not expand it, I will have no direct access to the paths and the copy paste will bring in non-editable paths;

- ❧ **Ungrouped it:** The brush shapes are attached to the path and bent to follow it;

- ❧ **Turned off Preview [Command+Y]:** so I could see the circle the brush artwork was attached to;

- ❧ **Deleted the original circle:** this is what would make the brush paths difficult to edit in InDesign;

- Copied from AI;

- Pasted into InDesign;

- Selected object with the Direct Selection tool and cleaned up the brush work a bit;

- Then I made and applied a gradient fill from Swatches.

- I checked Ignore Text Wrap in the Text Frame Options dialog box [Command+B]: and I added the type, breaking for sense and carefully spacing vertically.

InDesign's forte is graphic assembly

The whole procedure I just described took less than a minute—real time. Well, actually, two minutes because I was careful to set the type well. So, I was able to copy/paste a complex drawing into editable paths in InDesign in less than a minute. Obviously, getting editable pieces from Illustrator is quick and easy.

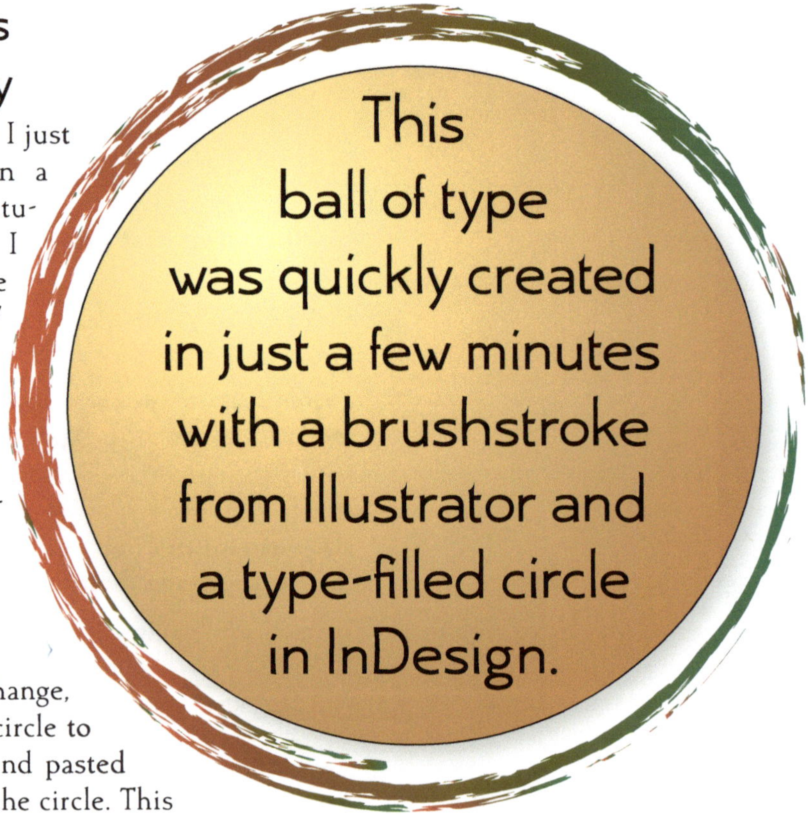

Using the brushstroke as a frame

To make a radical change, I modified the size of the circle to overlap the brushstroke, and pasted a picture of my home into the circle. This

This
ball of type
was quickly created
in just a few minutes
with a brushstroke
from Illustrator and
a type-filled circle
in InDesign.

took another minute—with the result you see on the next page. I added the type on top in another 20-30 seconds [the only glitch was that I had to set the new text frame to ignore text wraps as I had put a text wrap on the graphic automatically when I styled it with an object style]. Regardless, the whole thing was done in far less time than it took to write this explanation. It is dramatic if not too inspiring.

If I wanted a graphic I could use anywhere: All I would need to do is copy and paste the new graphic onto a new single page document, save it, and export it as a PDF [which I did]. If you are looking at this in an ebook, you can see it is in glorious 600-pixel-wide RGB color—rasterized in Photoshop and exported as a JPEG. For the B&W book, I could have rasterized into Photoshop and saved as a Grayscale PSD at 300 dpi. This is the vector PDF.

You can do graphics like this very quickly In fact, if you have the pieces at hand, any graphic of this nature can be done in less than a minute.

A Minnesota winter at home!

Fancy tables with inserted photos and complex typography can be created in a separate document and exported as a PDF to be used wherever needed at whatever size you need.

Graphic needs of the formats: Print, PDF, ePUB, & Kindle 8

The only other thing you need to understand about graphics is what works in which formats. I'm just going to list the four options and their requirements, best formats, and so on.

Greyscale print with color cover (Lulu & Createspace)

You need to be careful. This is digital printing and we are dependent upon the quality of equipment used by the vendors and the quality control exercised in their use. In general, I have had almost no problems with Lulu with print [but they are more expensive].

On the other hand, I have had many quality issues with Createspace. They are the 500 pound gorilla so we cannot ignore them. But, be careful and make sure your artwork is conservative. In all cases, the problem was solved by flattening Photoshop images or re-exporting PDFs limited to Acrobat 4 compatibility [which flattens all transparency]. In one case I had to rasterize a PDF at 300 dpi for a Createspace book. Don't argue. Just give them what they ask for.

> **Bitmap images:** 300 dpi grayscale PSDs, TIFFs, and PDFs. Lulu can handle layered PSDs with transparency. Createspace sometimes has trouble, although I've never had any issues with transparent backgrounds for either of them. Createspace sometimes drops color lighter than 10% (they have a tendency to print a little light).

❧ **Vector images:** PDFs, AIs, and EPSs. I use Acrobat 5 compatible PDFs for Lulu and Acrobat 4 compatible PDFs for Createspace. Lulu's printing of these images is much sharper. Createspace sometimes drops light tints (I suspect their raster image processor [RIP]is set up poorly).

Createspace's books are acceptable. Lulu's books are often excellent. This is on-demand digital printing.

Cover art

❧ **Lulu seems to prefer PDFs:** I use 300 dpi RGB bitmap images with vector lineart and type. Lulu provides a vector PDF of your ISBN artwork. You place it where needed. Their upload cover page gives you the necessary document size and spine widths. I assemble them in InDesign and export them with Acrobat 5 compatibility and have had no problems.

❧ **Createspace demands Photoshop PDF files:** Their recommended workflow starts with assembling a layered PSD on their template. Their PNG template has a guides layer showing bleed trim areas and maximum area for type. You are required to leave a specific area for the ISBN and they imprint the ISBN into that area.

They leave very little room for type on the spine and enforce their rules strictly. They

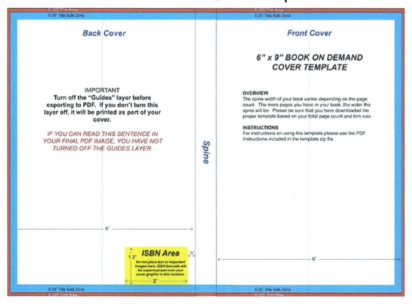

require 300 dpi RGB. Once you have all the type and images in place and saved as a layered PSD, you then flatten a copy and save it as a Photoshop PDF. They accept nothing else so far [mid-2013].

This required rasterization does soften the type (and often fattens it up quite a bit) and they can have problems printing rules thinner than three-quarter point (though normally they can print half-point rules with no problem). Make sure your type is large enough and clear enough to handle this.

Color printing throughout (Lulu & Createspace)

I haven't done much full-color printing. When I have, I've used Lulu. Every thing I said about greyscale printing still applies. Lulu works well with CMYK. My best guess is that Createspace likes RGB better (they might require it). This is my first full-color book with Createspace.

Downloadable PDFs (Lulu & Scribd)

Now that Lulu has separated the downloadable PDF from the printed version, there is no reason to avoid full-color. The same is true with Scribd. Lulu can easily handle everything that you can print. Scribd is geared more toward the Word user and has trouble with fancy stuff. For example, Scribd has trouble with paragraph rules, in general, and ruins rules with gradients. Scribd seems to be using a non-Adobe PDF reader, but I have no proof of that.

The bottom line is that you need to be much more careful proofing Scribd's online PDFs. Also Scribd does not seem to do well with sales. They are more geared to free stuff. But they can give you a lot of eyeballs. I've found they work very well for customized free previews of your books.

Lulu has always sold a lot of downloadable PDFs for me. That has slowed a lot now that they've moved PDFs to their own pages (they used to be a downloadable option on the print pages).

- **RGB color**

- **Vector if possible**

- **Go for 300 dpi bitmaps:** unless the file size gets too large. Scribd seems to have problems with files sizes much over 5 MB. Lulu does not seem to have those issues.

- **Acrobat 5 compatible:** seems to work for either

ePUBs and Kindle books will change radically in the next few years...

EPUBs (Lulu, Nook, and Kobo)

Think of this as Web design. It'll help conceptually. All graphics are bitmaps—no vectors allowed. The spec supports SVG, but that has not happened yet in reality.

- **Maximum image size:** 600x800 pixels: this has become the interim standard. In specific, image sizes are a bit more complex. The iPad full page image size is 600x860. The new iPad has a Retina display. I'm guessing 1200x1600 pixels works now [but that's over the possible two megapixel limit]. This is still all very fluid in the summer of 2013—so check *The Skilled Workman*]. Nook takes 600x730 pixels. Kobo uses 600x800.

- **RGB:** Use color to help

- **JPEGs or GIFs:** Supposedly PNGs work, as far as I know, but use the Save for Web option to help control file sizes.

- **Anchored objects above line for CC:** This preserves the graphics as well as possible.

Kindle KDP (Kindle Direct Publishing)

If you have an Amazon account, you have a KDP account to publish your books on Kindle. They have the most current requirements listed there. The new format is called Kindle Format Eight [KF8], and it was developed for Fire. Amazon supplies a free export KF8 Plug-in. At present, use the same basic options as you use in ePUBs

 The maximum image size is 127K: even a byte or two larger and Kindle will resize your image (with very bad results). It is so bad they warn us.

You can use embedded fonts with the Kindle Fire: This is a huge thing KF8 has brought about. The problem is that none of the tablet reader apps support this. The Kindle Export Plug-In for CS6 has really ramped up what can be done: Again many of these options only work on the Kindle Fire [though Amazon claims some of them work with the Kindle Touch]. For CC, I have been simply using Kindle Previewer to convert my ePUBs to Kindle KF8 files.

Do all graphics anchored with styles

Some times this is not possible—as in the little Tip graphic above. However, that little graphic is simply deleted in my ePUBs. Positioning your graphics in your print version with object styles makes it very easy to simply convert those styles to the inline graphics which are still required by ePUBs and Kindle books. As mentioned earlier, CC prefers all graphic to be anchored. Because of the minimal pixel width, I still suggest 600 pixels wide anchored slightly above line if the images contain useful information. For more decorative graphics, you can certainly try the other options. I know it is possible to hand-code your graphics as a percent width in divs.

Cover design

This area of graphic design has been going through major changes lately because of the nature of selling books online: Most of the traditional rules of cover design were geared toward displays at brick & mortar bookstores, magazine and book racks at supermarkets, and the large discount houses like Walmart, Sam's, Costco, and Target.

Until recently, the problem was that an author had no choice in cover designs if he or she was going with a traditional publisher. We are talking about self-publishing on-demand in this book. This means that virtually all your books will be sold online. Online sales mean that you need to have a cover design that reads well at very small sizes.

A list of thumbnail sizes in pixels

- **Lulu:** List size: 94 x 140
  Detail page size: 212 x 320
  Approximately 2x3 proportion but they usually specify a cover dimension of 612 x 792 pixels which is closer to a 3x4 proportion

- **Amazon:** List size: 60 x 90
  Detail page size: 164 x 242
  Their image specs are: Image dimensions of at least 500 by 800 pixels; A maximum of 2000 pixels on the longest side is preferred; Ideal height/width ratio of 1.6; Save at 72 dots per inch (dpi) for optimal viewing on the web. They currently ask for 1563x2500 pixels.

- **Nook:** List size: 128 x 192
  Detail page size: 300 x 450
  A 2x3 proportion but their specs are: "Please make sure that your cover image is a JPG file between 5KB and 2MB. The sides must

be between 750 pixels and 2000 pixels in length." Save at 72 dots per inch (dpi) for optimal viewing on the web [like 1300x1950]

❧ **Kobo:** List size: 84x112
Detail size:150x200
Display size: 220x293
I've just been uploading a 600x800 JPEG

❧ **iBooks:** Apple says they want 1440x1873

❧ **Scribd:** List size: 129 x 167

As you can see, all of these images are very small in size. Worse yet, you do not get much control of them. As you can see you upload them at wildly varying sizes. These uploaded images are then downsampled into very small sizes by the Website. So, what are we supposed to do? I'll admit I do not have a definitive answer yet. But you want to make them exactly to size with the pixels dimensions they ask for. We will talk about a technique for doing this in Photoshop and little bit.

What do we know for sure?

Many covers are close to 2x3: Amazon says the ideal is 2x3.2, a 6x9 book is 2x3 in proportion. So let's start with that.

The other standard is 3x4: We need to leave top and bottom margins which allow for adjustments: Lulu's ebook covers, for example, are specified to be 612x792. That divides out to 77% or about 3x4, as I mentioned. In practical terms, this means that I must take my 6" x 9" cover and reduce it to 6" x 8" to get the proper proportions. That's interesting because most people tell us that the maximum image size for an ePUB is 600 x 800 pixels [which is the same proportion].

We need color to the edges: If we leave a white background on the cover, the thumbnails get lost on the page. In fact, several of the companies specifically warn about covers with no background color.

At the small sizes the typography needs to be extremely readable and legible: This is not an problem solved by fancy, swirling type overlaying a complex photo. We really need to work at the legibility of the type. Basically we need to follow the dictum of billboard design: 8 words maximum, sharp contrast between the type and the background, nothing subtle, because all subtlety will be lost as you whiz by the billboard at 60 miles per hour.

Here are a couple of ideas:

- **One:** We can design the cover to be pure type reversed out of a dark background so we can freely resize it as necessary. The type block should be separate from the back ground so we can avoid type distortions as we resize the background to fit the various proportional needs.

- **Two:** We must carefully redesign the cover to fit each particular circumstance. This is going to be a particular problem if our book simply requires a photo or image on the cover. Obviously, any images used must be sharp enough and with enough contrast so the image is discernible at a half inch or so. Or, they must be so lacking in contrast that we can overlay the type without losing legibility.

The current solution

I now design my book covers as vector PDFs—always. If I have any bitmapped images like photos or other Photoshop artwork I make sure it does not compromise the legibility of the type. I leave large enough borders on all four sides so that I can crop the various covers as needed.

In Photoshop, I have set up custom presets in the Crop tool for Lulu, Kindle, Nook, Kobo, and the iBookstore. Then it is very easy to open my PDF into Photoshop with sufficient resolution to enable me to crop to size. It is never a perfect process, but it has greatly streamlined production of the various cover sizes necessary.

There is no easy solution

First of all we must reduce the copy to a minimum. Online covers are no place for lengthy epistles listing all the content. All there is really room for at these small sizes are the book title and your name. Even a subtitle can be a problem if it is too long. Let me show you a book I did two years ago and the two covers I finally used. It gave the start toward what we are talking about here.

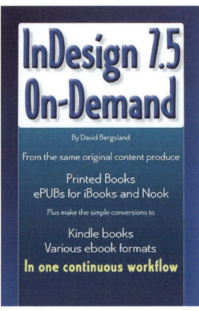
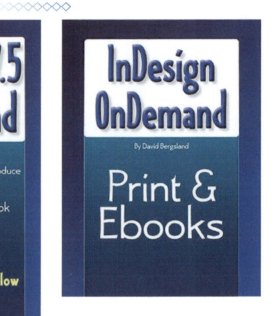

The cover on the left was the original designed for print. I really like it in color on the printed books. But in the online listings, it was always broken up very badly.

As you recall, even the large image on a Lulu detail page is only 212 x 320 pixels. At that size the color still looked very good, but the type was starting break up to the point where readability was bad & I risked poor reader reactions. Yes, the capture from Lulu on the right page looks a bit better than this on the computer screen—but not much. So, when I went to the ePUB version I did the image on the right above. Is that as pretty? No. But it is legible, readable, clear in concept, and probably produces a much better reader reaction when it is seen in a list on the screen.

InDesign 7.5 On-Demand

By David Bergsland

View this Author's Spotlight

Part of the Wattpad Marketplace

Paperback, 154 pages ☆☆☆☆☆ This item has not been rated yet

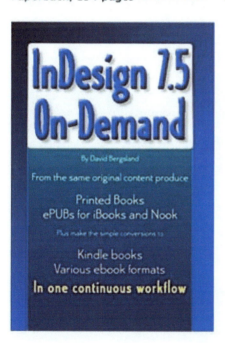

Price: **$12.95**

Ships in 3-5 business days

Help for authors & teachers publishing in the new millennium The focus of this book is very sharp. It is designed for people who are designing books and booklets with very limited capital and few personnel resources. It is a sharing of techniques for the new wave of author/pastor/teacher/designers who need to get their work published digitally & online.

Looking now I can see I should have made my name larger on all the covers—for I am selling my supposed expertise. In addition, I've been told that it's gauche and a sure sign of amateurism to use the word "By" in front of my name. I fully believe that is a mere fashion of the day, but what do I know? The main thing to recognize is that the author name is commonly more important than the subhead.

I now believe that the real solution is on the side of the ePUB version, but I would want to do a bit more to it and tweak the typography a bit. What is in no doubt is this, the second version has much more impact at small sizes.

Finally, make sure you look at the covers used by your competition. It's likely they'll show you a design style you should use to look appropriate. But the entire process of cover design is an art, not a science. No one has definitive answers—merely informed opinions.

However, amateur covers are obvious!

The number one mistake is made by adding all kinds of fancy trimmings to your type. Not only does it make the

type much harder to read, but all trained designers have been strongly told that NO ONE EVER does that. As a result, there are very few professional covers with type stylized like that. If it is, the type is carefully embossed, maybe beveled, using the minimal amount necessary to get the required effect. If the reader notices the type, the quality reaction to the cover is compromised.

Look at how easy it is to read the top sample. In color, the middle one is completely unreadable. But as you can see, even with careful embossing, the bottom example is also much more difficult to read. The extra space between the T and i make even the top title quite bad. Always kern your titles.

The point is simple. If there are any compromises in readability with the full size artwork, by the time you downsample for the tiny online images, that artwork will not be readable at all. In fact, as you can see to the left, even the plain type on the top is difficult to read because all the thin places of the font disappear at this 100-pixel-wide version. You must be sure that you look at your cover designs in a small size to determine the readability of your design. It is absolutely crucial.

Readability is the goal of book typography

In a similar vein, we need to mention that lowercase is more than twice as readable as all caps. Plus, lowercase can be made much larger on a cover because lowercase is much shorter than all caps.

Finally, the readability of the font is very important. In the two examples to the left, both the top version [set in Buddy] and the bottom version [set in Contenu] are far easier to read than the colored samples [set in Cutlass]. In fact, you should be able to see that Contenu is much more readable than Buddy. But you see color hurts these also.

Your name

In the same vein, your name needs to be very easy to read also. Your name is really your franchise. Your most recent book is simply a small addition to the platform.

Because all of our discovery is online, these things are crucial to our overall book design. None of it can be separated out. The cover, description, keywords, title, and so on are all equally important in the presentation of your book to your readers.

Now it is time to take a little break and go through the design of a cover. This was an actual project a year ago, and I am making no value judgment on it either good or bad. The techniques used are typical.

Don't forget the complex background problem

The bad type issues we've just covered are usually severely exacerbated by the complex photos upon which the type is dumped. If the background has a lot of complex high contrast detail, your type does not stand a chance—even if it is a good font set well. White type will not be seen in front of the light or white portions of the photo just as black type will not be seen over the dark areas of a photo. In image which is constantly going back and forth ruins any hope of type readability.

There is no way to fix this problem except to get a better photo. You might place a light or dark rectangle behind the type, but that usually ruins the photo. Just imagine poor Gus [the Corgi] if his picture was reduced to a cover icon 100 pixels wide.

A lot of your sales decisions will be based on the professionalism of your cover—like it or not!

Just as my poor Corgi disappears, so also will your headline disappear in a photo like this.

A cover tutorial

Something has come to my attention I should have noticed long ago: People do not have any idea how to apply effects to type because they have no experience with being able to add radical styling to live type.

Stylizing live type—only in InDesign

I forget that no one else allows you to even apply a gradient to live type. Illustrator requires you to convert your type to outlines and Photoshop requires you to rasterize it. InDesign lets you simply select it and apply a gradient—of any kind to the stroke and/or fill. In fact, in InDesign you can apply all the Effects available in InDesign—and that is quite a few. But this goes quite a bit further.

So, what I want to do is a small real world example to give you some ideas what can be done. I received a tentative proof of an idea for a book cover. The man who sent it is brand-new to designing in InDesign. He is actually doing very well—given his lack of training.

I critiqued it quite hard. I sent him back an annotated PDF with a dozen or so suggestions for improvement. I told him I thought it looked mid-century modern, and wondered if that would be effective for his audience (I have no idea as I have not looked into that market).

He wrote back that he was going for a similar look to one of his old King James Bibles with a black leather cover. I had no real idea what he was referring to, but I tossed off a quick idea to send back to him.

It turns out that stunned him, He had no concept of what could be done along these lines. I suggested some Photoshop tutorials and he went to look at some of them. His response was that he was amazed at what could be done, and he would let me know what he decided. He also suggested that I add this tutorial—so here goes.

HOLY BIBLE
MINOR PROPHETS

ספרכוננקדש

SIAPHERKONE
VERSION

One] Make new document with bleed

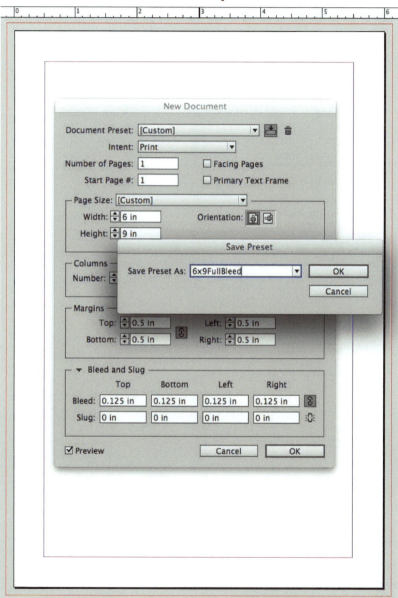

This is simple, but not often thought of before you do it awhile. I commonly make my graphics documents square and the same width as my column. But for this one I am doing a 6x9 cover and I want the ink to go to the edge of the printed cover. So, I need a bleed. You need to carefully look at the cover requirements at the various suppliers. If you have any questions write them or write me.

In addition, I made a New Document Preset by clicking on the Save Document Preset button. This opened the Save Preset As: dialog. I called the new preset: 6x9Full-Bleed—so I could recognize it in the list of presets.

Two] Add background layer for a template ◇◇◇◇◇◇◇

Next I added a new layer. As you can see I eventually used six layers. Into the new layer I placed the PDF proof

I was sent. Then I selected the actual graphic by clicking on the little selection donut in the center of the graphic window. I resized the PDF to fit the new margins of my document. I hit Command+ Option+ C to make the frame fit the resized content. I do not care at all that the original PDF is distorted quite a bit.

With the resized graphic selected, I went to the Effects panel and lightened it significantly by changing the opacity. I do not want the template graphic to confuse me as I draw on top of it. The final step was to lock the new layer. This gives me a guide to draw over—so I can keep the proportions correct. I am going with all new type, so that part of it doesn't matter at all.

Three] Find some leather

One of the things often forgotten when you are doing your own designs for the first time is the simple fact that your background does not have to be blank paper. You can add anything you like as a background color. If you look at

the cover of my *Writing In InDesign* book, for example, you will see that I have put a computer keyboard as a background image. I couldn't find what I liked, so I laid my laptop keyboard in the scanner and scanned it.

For this tutorial, my friend said his concept was an old KJV leather Bible. So I need an image of black leather. There are countless sources for images—and you can easily pay $300 for an excellent one. However, in this instance we are merely looking for texture. We will not get into copyright issues here, but you need to be sure you understand this. Use nothing without rights to it. So, where shall I look?

Sources for free images

- **Wikimedia Commons:** This visual adjunct to the open source online encyclopedia is filled with free images [well over 12,000,000 images at this point]. If you need an attribution, the page will tell you and give you the copy to use.

- **MorgueFile:** This site, MorgueFile, is not ghoulish. A morgue, in designers parlance, is the collection of images you build to use for reference as you draw you illustrations. This site has over 250,000 free images plus images for sale.

- **My camera:** If you can shoot photos, you have the best images you can use, because there is no question about copyright, at all. Just make sure you have any people used in your images sign a model release. You can Google for sample Model Release Forms. This will give you permission to use their image without problems.

For this tutorial I went to MorgueFile. I searched for leather textures and quickly found a photo of black leather which will work perfectly for what we need. I downloaded it. Opened it in Photoshop, and cleaned it up—saving it at 300 dpi for print use.

Four] Place leather in bottom layer

It will be the foundation for everything we build. At this point, I added a new layer (by clicking the little new layer button at the bottom of the panel) and dragged it just above the leather. I unlocked the original template and move it on top of the whole pile and relocked it. (I also deleted layer 6 which just held the labels for the capture a couple of pages ago. I may want to make it even more transparent so I can work through it and still see what I am doing.

I moved the leather into position, so it covered the entire page including the bleed. I then adjusted the handles of the frame enclosing the leather image to mask it to the exact size of the bleed. If I had needed to move the image around I would have selected the donut in the middle of the frame to select the actual graphic. The color of the handles should change so you can tell what you are working with as you move things around.

Five] Draw the top triangle

With the template on top and the leather on the bottom—both locked—it was a simple three click process to trace the triangle on the template with the Pen tool. I worked on a layer between the template and the leather. I choose a strong brilliant yellow-gold to color the triangle. I make it strong and bright because I was going to be making it transparent and additive to the leather texture. This process will radically tone down the color. If I do not make it strong enough, it will disappear when I adjust it.

Six] Adjust the transparency

With the new triangle selected and colored: I open the Effects panel and make the triangle 36% transparent—adjusting the look by eye. I also use the Multiply mode which takes the colors of the triangle and adds them to the under-lying leather texture. The result is something that looks like a transparent gold covering of the leather. To make it look more real I need to deboss it a little to make it look like it is slightly stamped into the surface of the leather.

Modes in Effects

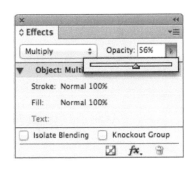

Modes were originally a Photoshop thing designed for working with layers. **Modes change how layers interact.** A mode will cause the selected object to interrelate to layers and objects below it. Let's look at some quick definitions.

Normal: What do you think? Everything remains normal and the layer does not interact with the layers below it. I think of it in terms of opaque overprinting, but then that is probably just my experience.

Multiply: This basically adds the color of each pixel of the layer to the colors of the pixels under that pixel. In other words, it makes the image darker. This is the way to darken and add detail to a very light image. Simply copy the image into a duplicate layer (drag the layer to the New Layer icon) and apply the Multiply mode. For severely light images, you might have to do this several times with varying opacities in the various layers. For some reason, several light transparent layers often work better than trying to do it all in one layer. It is an extremely handy mode. Shadows always multiply.

Screen: This mode is the opposite of Multiply. You can use this to lighten areas. I have seen images which looked totally black on the screen reveal astonishing detail through the application of Screened duplicate layers. This is also a good way to add highlights.

Overlay, Soft Light, and Hard Light: These three modes apply different combinations of Multiply and Screen using 50% gray as neutral. In other words, they apply effects to the highlights and shadows. Overlay, for example, uses the dark tones to darken the dark areas while the light tones lighten the light areas. Hard Light really exaggerates the highlights, often causing a *"plastic"* look. These modes can be used very well with filters like Emboss where the flat area is 50% gray.

Color Dodge or Burn: These two modes increase contrast by intensifying the hues or increasing the saturation (same thing). Color Dodge lightens as it brightens. Color Burn mainly deepens and intensifies the shadows.

Lighten and Darken: These modes work by comparing the pixels in the upper layer with those in the lower one. They do this channel by channel for all the channels. Lighten only makes changes when it finds a pixel in the upper layer that is lighter than the ones in the lower layer. Darken works oppositely by changing only pixels that are darker.

Difference: Here's one of those mathematical wonders. It compares the upper layer and the image below it using black as a neutral. If there is no difference in color between the two, those pixels are changed to black. It usually results in more saturated color, often psychedelic. It's great for professionally ugly stuff. As you can imagine I rarely use the filter.

Exclusion: This is a more subdued version of Difference that creates much less saturated colors (that is, they are grayed out). It is often even more ugly than Difference IMHO.

Hue, Saturation, and Luminosity: Here we have computer geek speak. For those of you with fine art training, these would be hue, saturation, and value. In each case, the mode takes that particular information from the overlying layer and applies it to the image beneath. Hue changes the colors only. Saturation changes the intensity only. Luminosity changes the value (or grayscale info) only.

Color: This mode applies both the hue and saturation — everything except the value.

The key is remembering that all of these modes can be applied to anything selected, and they can be applied transparently:

One thing where InDesign again demonstrates its superiority is that you can have separate modes and transparency for the fill, stroke, type, and/or the object as a whole. This is immensely helpful and no other application has anything that even comes close to this level of control. It gives you great power in manipulating text frames, as you can imagine.

They remain editable

Effects can always be edited: Just double-click on the *fx* in the Effects panel. They work with live type, text frames, graphic frames, and/or the contents of graphic frames. InDesign effects are immensely powerful and very useful to add graphic touches to your designs. Don't go overboard—only add them if they help your readers. Remember the adage: If you can't think of a good reason to use an image, color, or effect—don't do it!

But before I can do that there were two more things I needed to do.

First, I copied the new triangle and pasted. I clicked the flip vertically and the flip horizontally buttons in the Control bar—and dragged the triangle into position below.

Second, I dragged the layer with the transparent triangles down to the new layer icon and released it there. This made me a duplicate of the layer on top of the first one. As you will see this will intensify the color [because it is in multiply mode. Every time you do it, you basically double the intensity of the Multiply effect in its interaction with the leather texture. Then I selected both the triangle layer and its copy (by holding down the shift key and clicking on each layer). Finally I selected Merge Layers from the Option menu of the Layers panel. This saved the look I had developed and made it into one layer. As you can see opposite, this looks surprisingly realistic—even in grayscale.

Finally, I clicked the little *fx* button at the bottom of the Effects panel to add an effect to the selection. Then I chose Bevel and Emboss and made the settings you see below for a subliminal debossing into the leather.

I wanted it very subtle to keep it realistic: The only trick here is that the lower triangle is rotated, so I needed to make the embossing for it up instead of down to keep the shadows on the right edges. It's keeping track of the little details like this which makes the illusion realistic.

Effects

Settings for: Object

Transparency
- ☐ Drop Shadow
- ☐ Inner Shadow
- ☐ Outer Glow
- ☐ Inner Glow
- ☑ Bevel and Emboss
- ☐ Satin
- ☐ Basic Feather
- ☐ Directional Feather
- ☐ Gradient Feather

OBJECT: Multiply 56%; Bevel and Emboss
STROKE: Normal 100%; (no effects)
FILL: Normal 100%; (no effects)

☐ Preview

Bevel and Emboss

Structure
Style: Inner Bevel Size: 0.04 in
Technique: Smooth Soften: 0 in
Direction: Down Depth: 100%

Shading
Angle: 120° Altitude: 30°
☐ Use Global Light
Highlight: Screen Opacity: 75%
Shadow: Multiply Opacity: 75%

Cancel OK

Seven] Set the type

I added the type into the two triangles. I carefully kerned it to get the letter-spacing looking professional. Then I added a slight deboss (emboss down, remember). It was still not enough to set off the type. So, I added a quarter-point white stroke to the type. This is so thin that it is almost subliminal—but you'll be surprised at how much it makes the type pop out.

The type still did not have enough contrast to I went to the leather layer and lightened that a bit. I made it 75%

opaque (which I later changed to 80%). I think it would work better in color if I made the leather brown also.

Eight] Add the Hebrew

I saved the type into a separate file in Illustrator where I could simply copy/paste the type into the InDesign document. If I had the font I could have set it in Hebrew—but all I had was the original PDF. So I dropped it in and it looked like what you see to the right.

The next thing I wanted to do was give the Hebrew an illusion of metal—gold in the color version.

I started the process by making the type a pale yellow. For, as you know, gold is basically a yellow. It needs to be a clean yellow with no blue or greenish hints. I used a new swatch set at 0 cyan, 20 magenta, 90 yellow 0 black. After I colored the type this color, I set it for a 35% tint.

Next I add a set of effects by clicking on the *fx* button at the button of the

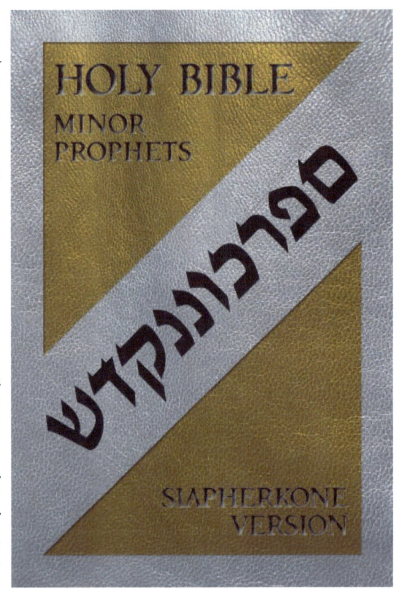

Effects panel. When it opens, I choose Bevel and Emboss set to 100%, up, and the rest of the settings you see below. In addition, as you can see I added a slight softening with the Satin effect. Finally I added a little bit of inner shadowing. The only thing I should mention is adding colors to the highlights and shadows. If you look closely at the capture below, you'll notice that I changed the highlight and shadows to a gold and brown respectively.

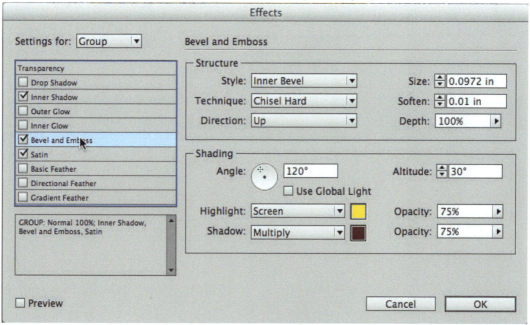

I did the same thing with the inner shadow. When I clicked on the colored box to the right of the mode popup, I opened the Effect Color dialog. It opens to Swatches, but you can change this to RGB or CMYK and pick the color you like. You can see I picked a warm brown: 15 cyan, 64 magenta, 100 yellow, and 20 black.

The final result looks pretty good, considering it was all done in InDesign. Yes, I can be much more fancy in

Photoshop. But it is not necessary. As you can see below, this will do fine.

Of course, Photoshop does kick it up a notch. But it's not necessary. [Between you and me, it's not as easily readable. Plus, it does not convincingly lie on the page.]

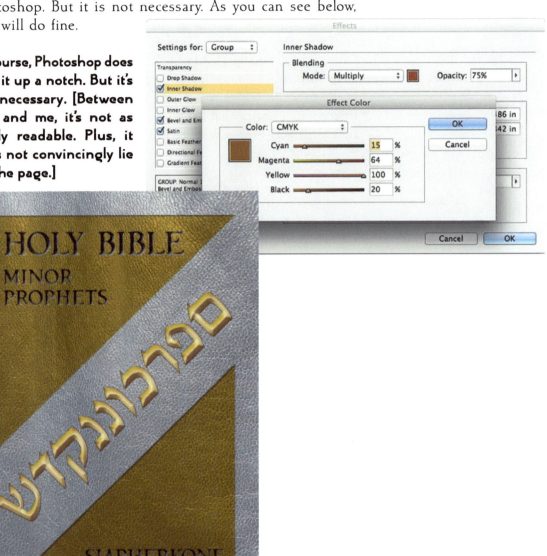

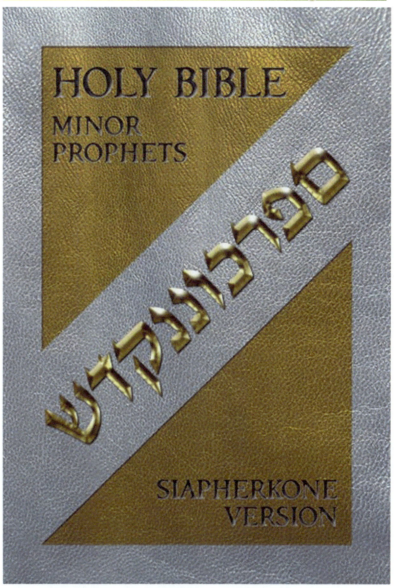

The final stage in cover design, is to rasterize it as a 300 dpi grayscale image which you can use on your title page. The only problem you will have is that your margins are much more narrow proportionally than your page size. You will have to come up with a solution for that issue.

The other difference with the title page image is that, in most cases, you will be adding the publishing house logo and the locations where it will be published. This is not absolutely essential, but it is commonplace. It is one of the places you can make your book look more professional.

For most of us this grayscale title image will be for a book printed by Createspace. Make sure you leave a three-quarter inch margin at the gutter or Createspace will flag it. Other than that all you have to do is rasterize the small JPEG's needed for your blog, FaceBook postings, and situations like that.

For the rest of the publishing process get

Practical, Professional Self-Publishing Handbook

All the updated info from this graphics book & PPSH will also be included in the new 3rd edition of:

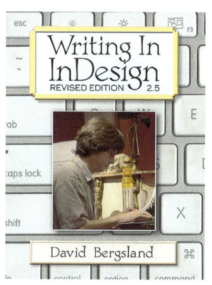

Writing In InDesign Edition 3

This is where my heart is. Book design and publishing for the self-publisher is my passion. I was trained as a fine artist, but creating books is what gets me excited. It's a wonderful creative project to take a book from concept to the reader. That's the new paradigm of publishing and you can learn how to do it.

Edition 3 is due out around New Year 2014. If you think of anything else you want me to cover, please just email me at the publishing house: david@radiqx.com

www.ingramcontent.com/pod-product-compliance
Lightning Source LLC
Chambersburg PA
CBHW041427050326
40689CB00003B/687